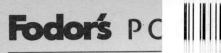

Fodor's PO

kyōto

first edition

Excerpted from *Fodor's Japan*

fodor's travel publications
new york • toronto • london • sydney • auckland
www.fodors.com

contents

maps

on the road with fodor's

THE MORE YOU KNOW BEFORE YOU GO, the better your trip will be. Kyōto's loveliest temple could be just around the corner from your hotel, but if you don't know it's there, it might as well be across the globe. That's where this guidebook and our Web site, Fodors.com, come in. Our editors work hard to give you useful, on-target information. Their efforts begin with finding the best contributors—people with good judgment and broad travel experience—the people you'd poll for tips yourself if you knew them.

Kyōto updater **Lauren Sheridan** spent more than five years living and studying at various universities in Kyōto. A recipient of the prestigious Japanese Ministry of Education Research scholarship, she studied at Kyōto University for two years. Her research topic focused on the lives of women working in the entertainment district of Gion. She now enjoys studying about Kyōto's traditional crafts, such as *temari* (balls decorated with brightly colored silk thread in complex geometric shapes) and *kyō-ningyō* (display dolls).

Don't Forget to Write

Your experience—positive and negative—matters to us. We follow up on all suggestions, so be sure to contact the Kyōto editor at editors@fodors.com or c/o Fodor's, 280 Park Avenue, 10th Floor, New York, NY 10017. Have a wonderful trip!

Karen Cure
Editorial Director

HOKKAIDO

Rebun-to
Rishiri-to
Wakkanai

Monbetsu

Abashiri

Shiretoko
Peninsula

Asahigawa

Kunashiri
Island

Sapporo

Oshima
Peninsula

Noboribetsu

Kushiro

Hakodate

Train Ferry

Oki
Islands

N

Matsue

Tottori

Tsushima

Hagi

Iki Island

Yamaguchi

Hiroshima

Okayama

Takamatsu

Kobe

Fukuoka

Seto Nai-kai

Osaka

Awaji
Island

Matsuyama

Goto
Islands

Beppu

Oita

Tokushima

Wakayama

Aso

Koya

Nagasaki

Amakusa
Islands

Kumamoto

Uwajima

Kochi

Kii
Peninsula

Shingu

Shimo-Koshiki
Island

S H I K O K U

KYUSHU

Miyazaki

Kagoshima

Kuchinoerabu
Island

Yaku
Island

Tanega
Island

HOKKAIDO
(see inset)

Hakodate

Tsugaru
Peninsula

Shimokita
Peninsula

Aomori

Akita   Morioka

Tono

Tsuruoka

Sado
Island

Niigata

Yamagata

Sendai

Fukushima

Noto
Peninsula

Kanazawa

Toyama

Nikko

Utsunomiya

Fukui

Nagano

Takayama

Matsumoto

Maebashi

Oyama

Mito

Maibara

Kofu

Kyoto

Gifu

Tokyo

Osaka   Nara   Tsu

Nagoya

Chiba

Fuji-san

Yokohama

Kamakura

Shizuoka

Izu
Peninsula

yama
Koya-san

Ise

Oshima

Shingu

HONSHU

TAIHEIYO
(Pacific Ocean)

KEY
JR Trains
Shinkansen
(Bullet Train)
Roads

0   50 miles
0   75 km

kyōto

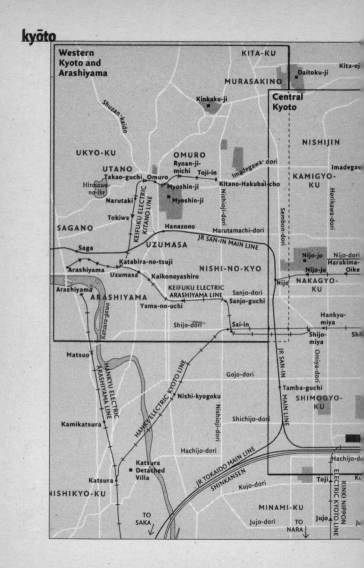

Western
Kyoto and
Arashiyama

KITA-KU

Kita-oji

Daitoku-ji

MURASAKINO

Kinkaku-ji

Central
Kyoto

NISHIJIN

Imadegaw

UKYO-KU

OMURO

Ryoan-ji-
michi

Imadegawa-dori

KAMIGYO-
KU

Horikawa-dori

UTANO

Takao-guchi   Omuro

Toji-in

Myoshin-ji

Kitano-Hakubai-cho

Hirosawa-
no-ike

Narutaki

Myoshin-ji

Nishioji-dori

Sembon-dori

Tokiwa

SAGANO

Hanazono

Marutamachi-dori

Nijo-dori

Saga

UZUMASA

JR SAN-IN MAIN LINE

Nijo-jo

Nijo-jo

Harakima-
Oike

NISHI-NO-KYO

Arashiyama

Katabira-no-tsuji

Nijo

NAKAGYO-
KU

Arashiyama

Uzumasa

Kaikonoyashiro

KEIFUKU ELECTRIC
KITANO LINE

KEIFUKU ELECTRIC
ARASHIYAMA LINE

Sanjo-dori

Hankyu-
miya

ARASHIYAMA

Yama-no-uchi

Sanjo-guchi

Shijo-dori

Sai-in

Shijo-
miya

Shi

Omiya-dori

Matsuo

Gojo-dori

JR SAN-IN MAIN LINE

Tamba-guchi

SHIMOGYO-
KU

HANKYU ELECTRIC
KYOTO LINE

HANKYU ELECTRIC
ARASHIYAMA LINE

Nishi-kyogoku

Nishioji-dori

Shichijo-dori

Kamikatsura

Hachijo-dori

Hachijo-d

Katsura
Detached
Villa

Toji

Ku

Katsura

JR TOKAIDO MAIN LINE

SHINKANSEN

Kujo-dori

KINKI NIPPON
ELECTRIC KYOTO LINE

NISHIKYO-KU

MINAMI-KU

TO
SAKA

Jujo-dori

TO
NARA

Jujo

Ju

Botanical Garden
Kamigamo Jinja
Kita-oji-dori
Kita-oji
SHIMOGAMO

0   1 mile
0   1 km

N

EIZAN ELECT.
KURANA LINE   Ichijo-ji
EIZAN ELECT.   **KITA-**
EIZAN LINE   **SHIRAKAWA**

Kurama-guchi
Chayama
TAKANO

Mt. Uryu

SUBWAY

Eastern Kyoto

Mototanaka   **SAKYO-KU**

degawa

Kyoto Imperial Palace

Demachi-Yanagi
Imadegawa-dori
Demachi-Yanagi
Keihan

Ginkaku-ji

Nyoigatake

Maruta-machi
Maruta-machi-dori

Heian Jing

OKAZAKI

Maruta-machi
o-dori
akima-
Oike

Karasuma-Oike

Oike-dori

Higashiyama   Sanjo-dori
Karasuma
Shijo   Shijo-dori
Sanjo   Keishin-Sanjo   Keage
Keihan   **TOZAI LINE**
AWATAGUCHI

KEY

—— JR Trains
—— Shinkansen (Bullet Train)
- - - Subway
+—+ Private rail line

Kawara-machi
Shijo
Keihan
GION

Kujo-yama

YAMASHINA-KU

TO TOKYO

Gojo-dori
Gojo   Gojo
Kiyomizu-dera
Mt. Kiyomizu
HIGASHIYAMA-KU
Mt. Kazan

Hino-oka   Misasagi
Yamashina
Keihan-Yamashina   Shinomiya

Shichijo

Kyoto Eki

Mt. Rokujo

JR TOKAIDO MAIN LINE

SHINKANSEN

KANSAI REGION

Kyoto
Kobe
Osaka
Lake Biwa

chijo-dori
Kujo-dori   Tofukuji
KINKI NIPPON

KEIHAN ELECTRIC MAIN LINE

Osaka Bay
Nara

Jujo-dori   Tobakaido

Yoshino-san
Koya-san

kyōto

In This Chapter

introducing kyōto

KYŌTO'S HISTORY IS FULL OF CONTRADICTIONS: famine and prosperity, war and peace, calamity and tranquillity. Although the city was Japan's capital for more than 10 centuries, the real center of political power was often elsewhere, be it Kamakura (1192–1333) or Edo (1603–1868). Such was Kyōto's decline in the 17th and 18th centuries that when the power of the government was returned from the shōguns to the emperor, he moved his capital and imperial court to Edo, renaming it Tōkyō. Though that move may have pained Kyōto residents, it actually saved the city from destruction. Although most major cities in Japan were bombed flat in World War II, Kyōto survived. And where old quarters of Tōkyō have been replaced with characterless modern buildings— a fate that Kyōto has shared in part—much of the city's wooden architecture of the past still stands.

Until 710 Japan's capital was moved to a new location with the succession of each new emperor. When it was decided that the expense of this continuous movement had become overly bloated with the size of the court and the number of administrators, Nara was chosen as the permanent capital. Its life as the capital lasted only 74 years, during which time Buddhists rallied for, and achieved, tremendous political power. In an effort to thwart them, Emperor Kammu moved the capital in 784 to Nagaoka, leaving the Buddhists behind in their elaborate temples. Within 10 years, Kammu decided that Kyōto (then called Uda) was better suited for his capital. Poets were asked to compose verse about Uda, and invariably they included the phrase *Heian-kyō*, meaning "Capital of Peace," reflecting the hope and desire of the time.

For 1,074 years, Kyōto remained the capital, though at times only in name. From 794 to the end of the 12th century, the city flourished under imperial rule. Japan's culture started to grow independent of Chinese influences and to develop its unique characteristics. Unfortunately, the use of wood for construction, coupled with Japan's two primordial enemies, fire and earthquakes, has destroyed all the buildings from this era, except Byōdō-in in Uji. The short life span of a building in the 11th century is exemplified by the Imperial Palace, which burned down 14 times in 122 years. As if natural disasters were not enough, imperial power waned in the 12th century. A period of shogunal rule followed, but each shōgun's reign was tenuous. By the 15th century civil wars tore the country apart. Many of Kyōto's buildings were destroyed or looted.

The Ōnin Civil War (1467–77) was particularly devastating for Kyōto. Two feudal lords, Yamana and Hosokawa, disputed who should succeed the reigning shōgun. Yamana camped in the western part of the city with 90,000 troops, and Hosokawa settled in the eastern part with 100,000 troops. Central Kyōto was the battlefield.

Not until the end of the 16th century, when Japan was brought together by the might of Nobunaga Oda and Hideyoshi Toyotomi, did Japan settle down. This period was soon followed by the usurpation of power by Ieyasu Tokugawa, founder of the Tokugawa Shogunate, which lasted for the next 264 years. Tokugawa moved the political center of the country to Edo, current-day Tōkyō. Kyōto did remain the imperial capital—the emperor being little more than a figurehead—and the first three Tokugawa shōguns paid homage to it by restoring old temples and building new villas. In the first half of the 17th century, this was yet another show of Tokugawa power. Much of what you see in Kyōto dates from this period.

Steeped in history and tradition, Kyōto has in many ways been the cradle of Japanese culture, especially with its courtly aesthetic pastimes, such as moon-viewing parties and tea ceremonies. A stroll through Kyōto today is a walk through 11 centuries of Japanese history. The city has been swept into the modern industrialized world with the rest of Japan—plate-glass windows, held in place by girders and ferroconcrete, dominate central Kyōto. Elderly women, however, continue to wear kimonos as they make their way slowly along the canal walkways. Geisha still entertain, albeit at prices out of reach for most visitors. Sixteen hundred temples and several hundred shrines surround central Kyōto. There's a lot to see, to say the least, so it's best to keep this in mind and not run yourself ragged. Balance a morning at temples and museums with an afternoon in traditional shops and a morning at the market with the rest of the day in Arashiyama or at one of the imperial villas.

Kyōto Glossary

Key Japanese words and suffixes for this book include -bashi (bridge), bijutsukan (art museum), -chō (street or block), -chōme (street), -den (hall), -dō (temple or shrine), dōri (street), eki (train station), gaijin (foreigner), -gawa or -kawa (river), -gū (Shintō shrine), hakubutsukan (museum), higashi (east), -in (Buddhist temple), -ji (temple), jingū or jinja (Shintō shrine), -jō (castle), kado (street corner), kita (north), kōen (park), -ku (section or ward), machi (town), matsuri (festival), michi (street), minami (south), -mon (gate), nishi (west), ryokan (traditional inn), sakura (cherry blossoms), -shi (city or municipality), Shinkansen (bullet train, literally "new trunk line"), taisha (Shintō shrine), torii ("to-ree-ee," gate), yama (mountain), and -zan (mountain, as in Hiei-zan, Mt. Hiei).

PLEASURES AND PASTIMES

Although Tōkyō has been the imperial capital since 1868, Kyōto—which wore the crown for the 10 centuries before—is still the classic Japanese city. The traditional arts, crafts, customs, language, and literature were all born, raised, and refined here. Kyōto has the matchless villas, the incomparable gardens, the magnificent temples and shrines. And Kyōto has the most artful Japanese cuisine.

ARCHITECTURE

No other city in Japan has such a glorious array of religious architecture. Over its 1,200-year history the city has accumulated more than 1,600 Buddhist temples (30 of which are the headquarters for major sects spread throughout Japan), 200 Shintō shrines, and three imperial palaces. All of these vying for your attention can be a bit daunting, but there are clear standouts, places at which you can get the best of Japan's harmonious, graceful architectural styles without having to dash back and forth with a checklist.

CRAFTS

Temples, shrines, gardens, and the quintessential elements of Japanese culture are all part of Kyōto's appeal, but you can't take them home with you. You can, however, pack up a few *omiyage* (mementos)—the take-home gifts for which this city is famous. The ancient craftsmen of Kyōto served the imperial court for more than 1,000 years, and the prefix *kyō-* before a craft is synonymous with fine craftsmanship. The wares you will find in Kyōto are, for their superb artistry and refinement, among the world's finest.

Kyō-ningyō, exquisite display dolls, have been made in Kyōto since the 9th century. Constructed of wood coated with white shell paste and clothed in elaborate, miniature patterned-silk brocades, Kyōto dolls are considered the finest in Japan. Kyōto is also known for fine ceramic dolls and *Kyō-gangu*, its local varieties of folk toys.

Kyō-*sensu* are embellished folding fans used as accoutrements in Nō theater, tea ceremonies, and Japanese dance. They also have a practical use—to keep you cool. Unlike other Japanese crafts, which have their origins in Tang dynasty China, the folding fan originated in Kyōto.

Kyō-*shikki* refers to Kyōto lacquerware, which also has its roots in the 9th century. The making of lacquerware, adopted from the Chinese, is a delicate process requiring patience and skill. Finished lacquerware products range from furniture to spoons and bowls, which are carved from cypress, cedar, or horse-chestnut wood. These pieces have a brilliant luster; some designs are decorated with gold leaf and inlaid mother-of-pearl.

Kyō-*yaki* is the general term applied to ceramics made in local kilns; the most popular ware is from Kyōto's Kiyomizu district. Often colorfully hand-painted in blue, red, and green on white, these elegantly shaped teacups, bowls, and vases are thrown on potters' wheels in the Kiyomizu district and in Kiyomizu-danchi in Yamashina. Streets leading up to Kiyomizu-dera—Chawan-zaka, Sannen-zaka, and Ninen-zaka—are sprinkled with kyō-yaki shops.

Kyō-*yuzen* is a paste-resist silk-dyeing technique developed by 17th-century dyer Yuzen Miyazaki. Fantastic designs are created on plain white silk pieces through the process of either *tegaki yuzen* (hand-painting) or *kata yuzen* (stenciling).

Nishijin-ori is the weaving of silk. Nishijin refers to a Kyōto district producing the best silk textiles in all of Japan, which are used to make kimonos. Walk along the narrow backstreets of Nishijin and listen to the persistently rhythmic looms.

DINING

Kyōto is home to the nation's haute cuisine, *kaiseki ryōri*, the elegant full-course meal that was originally intended to be served with the tea ceremony. More than a meal, this is a culinary event that engages all the senses. An atmosphere is created in which the meal is to be experienced. A poem in calligraphy on a hanging scroll and flowers in an alcove set a seasonal theme, a motif picked up in the pattern of the dishware chosen for an evening. The colors and shapes of the vessels complement the foods served on them. The visual harmony presented is as vital as the balance and variety of flavors of the foods themselves, for which the ultimate criterion is freshness. The finest ryōtei (high-class Japanese restaurants) will never serve a fish or vegetable out of its proper season—no matter how marvelous a winter melon today's modern greenhouses can guarantee. Melons are for rejoicing in summer's bounty . . . period.

GARDENS

Simplicity and symbolism are the perfected goals of Kyōto's temple gardens. The tea garden at Kinkaku-ji, with stepping stones paving the way through manicured grounds, sets the spirit at rest. The timeless arrangement of the karesansui (dry-garden) sand and rocks at Ryōan-ji is an eternal quest for completeness. The tree-shrouded gardens at Jakkō-in feed melancholy.

LODGING

Considering the huge numbers of people who visit Kyōto, the city has a surprising dearth of good hotels. Except for pricey ryokan, the hotels do not compare with their counterparts in Ōsaka or Tōkyō. So don't expect too much, and you won't be disappointed. As for the very expensive ryokans, $500–$600 per night will bring genteel attention, an elegant dinner, and the classical harmony of the tatami rooms. No other Japanese city can compete with Kyōto for style and grace, but it is not always given freely to foreigners. Remember that it helps to have a Japanese person make a reservation for you at a ryokan, unless you can speak Japanese yourself. The idea is to let the ryokan know that you understand the customs of staying at traditional inns.

MATSURI (FESTIVALS)

Kyōto's festival calendar includes five spectacular events: the Aoi, Gion, Jidai, and the Daimon-ji and Kurama fire matsuri.

Dating from the 6th century, the **Aoi Festival,** also known as the Hollyhock Festival, takes place on May 15. An "imperial" procession of 300 courtiers starts from the Imperial Palace and makes its way to Shimogamo Jinja to pray for the prosperity of the city. Today's participants are local Kyōtoites. The **Gion Festival,** which dates from the 9th century, is perhaps Kyōto's most popular festival. For two days in mid-July, 29 huge floats sail along downtown streets and make their way to Yasaka Jinja to thank the gods for protection from a pestilence that once ravaged the city. For the **Daimon-ji Gozan Okuribi** on August 16, huge bonfires in the shape of kanji characters illuminate five of the mountains that surround Kyōto. Dress in a cool *yukata* (cotton robe) and walk down to the banks of the Kamo-gawa to view this spectacular summer sight, or catch all five fires from the rooftop of your hotel downtown or a spot in Funaoka-yama or Yoshida-yama parks. There are dances as well as the floating of lanterns in Arashiyama (the western district). On October 22, the **Jidai Festival,** the Festival of Eras, features a colorful costume procession of fashions from the 8th through 19th centuries. The procession begins at the Imperial Palace and winds up at Heian Jinja. More than 2,000 Kyōtoites voluntarily participate in this festival, which dates to 1895. On October 22, the **Kurama Fire Festival,** at Kurama Shrine, involves a roaring bonfire and a rowdy portable shrine procession that makes its way through the narrow streets of the small village in the northern suburbs of Kyōto. If you catch a spark, it is believed to bring good luck.

Smart Sightseeings

Savvy travelers and others who take their sightseeing seriously have skills worth knowing about.

DON'T PLAN YOUR VISIT IN YOUR HOTEL ROOM Don't wait until you pull into town to decide how to spend your days. It's inevitable that there will be much more to see and do than you'll have time for: choose sights in advance.

ORGANIZE YOUR TOURING Note the places that most interest you on a map, and visit places that are near each other during the same morning or afternoon.

START THE DAY WELL EQUIPPED Leave your hotel in the morning with everything you need for the day—maps, medicines, extra film, your guidebook, rain gear, and another layer of clothing in case the weather turns cooler.

TOUR MUSEUMS EARLY If you're there when the doors open you'll have an intimate experience of the collection.

EASY DOES IT See museums in the mornings, when you're fresh, and visit sit-down attractions later on. Take breaks before you need them.

STRIKE UP A CONVERSATION Only curmudgeons don't respond to a smile and a polite request for information. Most people appreciate your interest in their home town. And your conversations may end up being your most vivid memories.

GET LOST When you do, you never know what you'll find—but you can count on it being memorable. Use your guidebook to help you get back on track. Build wandering-around time into every day.

QUIT BEFORE YOU'RE TIRED There's no point in seeing that one extra sight if you're too exhausted to enjoy it.

TAKE YOUR MOTHER'S ADVICE Go to the bathroom when you have the chance. You never know what lies ahead.

MUSEUMS

Kyōto and Tōkyō are rivals for the role as the nation's leading repository of culture. Certainly Kyōto wins hands down for its traditional and courtly treasures. You won't get this feeling from walking the busy, congested streets of modern downtown, but a step into any of the nine major museums will sweep you back to the days of refinement and artistic perfection.

SHOPPING

Perhaps even more than Tōkyō, Kyōto is the Japanese city in which to shop for gifts to take home. As Japan's self-proclaimed cultural capital, Kyōto has no shortage of art and antiques shops. Folk crafts from surrounding regions are brought into town for shops to sell. Secondhand kimonos can be a steal at $50, after image-conscious Japanese discard them for new ones priced in the thousands of dollars. Ceramics and woven bamboo make great souvenirs, and if you're looking for odds and ends, there are always the flea markets.

In This Chapter

Updated by Lauren Sheridan

here and there

MOST OF KYŌTO'S INTERESTING SIGHTS are north of Kyōto Eki. Think of this northern sector as three rectangular areas abutting each other.

The middle rectangle fronts the exit of Kyōto Eki. This is central Kyōto. Here are the hotels, the business district, the Ponto-chō geisha district, and the Kiya-machi entertainment district. Central Kyōto also contains one of the oldest city temples, Tōji; the rebuilt Imperial Palace; and Nijō-jō, the onetime Kyōto abode of the Tokugawa shōguns. Eastern Kyōto, Higashiyama, is chockablock with temples and shrines, among them Ginkaku-ji, Heian Jingū, and Kiyomizu-dera. Gion—a traditional shopping neighborhood by day and a geisha entertainment district by night—is also here. You could easily fill two days visiting eastern Kyōto. Western Kyōto includes the temples Ryōan-ji and Kinkaku-ji, and Katsura Rikyū, a bit south.

You could skim over these three areas, so crowded with historical attractions, in three days. However, two other areas have major sights to lure you. West of the western district is Arashiyama, with its temple, Tenryū-ji. And north of central Kyōto are Hiei-zan and the suburb of Ōhara, where the poignant story of Kenreimonin takes place at Jakkō-in.

Kyōto's sights spread over a wide area, but many of them are clustered together, and you can walk from one to another. Where the sights are not near each other, you can use Kyōto's buses, which run on a grid pattern that is easy to follow. Pick up route maps at the JNTO (Japan National Tourist Organization) office. The following exploring sections keep to the divisions described above so as to allow walking from one sight to another. However, notwithstanding traffic and armed with a bus map, you could cross and recross Kyōto without too much difficulty, stringing together sights of your own choosing.

Unlike other Japanese cities, Kyōto was modeled on the grid pattern of the Chinese city of Xian. Accordingly, addresses in the city are organized differently than in other parts of the country. Residents will assure you that this makes the city easier to navigate; confounded tourists may disagree. Many of the streets are named and east–west streets are numbered—the *san* in Sanjō-dōri, for example, means "three." *Nishi-iru* means "to the west," *higashi-iru*, "to the east." *Agaru* is "to the north" and *sagaru* "to the south." These directions are normally given in relation to the closest intersection. Thus the ryokan Daimonjiya's address, Nishi-Iru, Kawara-machi-Sanjō, means "to the west of the junction of Kawara-machi Street and Sanjō (Third Street)."

Admission to Kyōto sights adds up. Over the course of three days, charges of ¥400–¥500 at each sight can easily come to $100 per person.

EASTERN KYŌTO

Start your Kyōto odyssey in Higashiyama (literally, "Eastern Mountain"). If you have time to visit only one district, this is the one. There's more to see here than you could cover comfortably in one day, so pick and choose from the following tour according to your interests.

Numbers in the text correspond to numbers in the margin and on the Eastern Kyōto map.

A Good Walk

GINKAKU-JI ① is one of Kyōto's most famous sights, a wonderful villa turned temple. To get here, take Bus 5 from Kyōto Eki to the Ginkaku-ji-michi bus stop. Walk on the street along the canal, going east. A hundred yards after the street crosses a north–south canal, you'll see **Hakusha Son-sō Garden**, a small villa with an impeccable garden, and then Ginkaku-ji. You'll want to spend a good half hour here soaking up the atmosphere. When you can tear yourself away from Ginkaku-ji, retrace your steps on the entrance road until you reach, on your left, the **PATH OF PHILOSOPHY** ②, which follows alongside the canal. At the first large bridge as you walk south, turn off the path, cross the canal, and take the road east to the modest **HŌNEN-IN** ③, with its thatched roof and quiet park. After Hōnen-in, return to the Path of Philosophy and continue south. In 15 minutes or so you'll reach, on your left, the temple **EIKAN-DŌ** ④. If you cross the street from Eikan-dō and continue south, you'll see, on the right, the **NOMURA BIJUTSUKAN** ⑤, a museum with a private collection of Japanese art.

If the day is close to an end, walk from the Nomura Bijutsukan to Heian Jingū and the Kyōto Handicraft Center, on Maruta-machi-dōri behind it. If not, continue this tour, which returns shortly to Heian Jingū.

Walk south from Nomura Bijutsukan and follow the main path. On your left will be **NANZEN-JI** ⑥, headquarters of the Rinzai sect of Zen Buddhism, with its classic triple gate, San-mon. See also Nanzen-in, a smaller temple within Nanzen-ji. Outside the main gate of Nanzen-ji but still within the complex, take the side street to the left, and you will come to **KONCHI-IN** ⑦, with its pair of excellent gardens. At the intersection at the foot of the road to Nanzen-ji, you'll see the expansive grounds of the **KYŌTO INTERNATIONAL COMMUNITY HOUSE** ⑧, across the street to the left. Walk back to the main road to Nanzen-ji and turn left. Cross at the traffic light to get to the Meiji-period

eastern kyōto

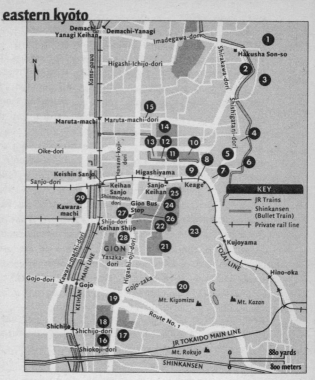

MURIN-AN GARDEN ⑨, whose entrance is on a side road half a block east. Walk back north toward the canal and turn left. If you were to cross the canal at the first right, you would be at the **DŌBUTSU-EN** ⑩, Kyōto's zoo. But there's no pressing reason to visit it, unless you have children in tow. If you skip the zoo, continue to the next right and cross the bridge over the canal. You'll see an immense vermilion torii that acts as a distant entry for Heian Jingū. There are two museums flanking the other side of the torii, the **KYŌTO-SHI BIJUTSUKAN** ⑪, on your right, and the **KINDAI BIJUTSUKAN** ⑫, on your left. Close by is the **DENTŌ SANGYŌ KAIKAN** ⑬, which exhibits traditional Kyōto crafts. Pass through the torri to get to the **HEIAN JINGŪ** ⑭.

If the urge comes on to do some shopping, cross Maruta-machi-dōri and turn left, and you'll come to the **KYŌTO HANDICRAFT CENTER** ⑮. At the crossroads of Maruta-machi-dōri and Higashi-ōji-dōri, west of the handicraft center, is the Kumano Jinja-mae bus stop. If you've had enough sightseeing for one day, take Bus 202 or 206 five stops south on Higashi-ōji-dōri to the Gion bus stop; here, some of the city's best restaurants and bars are at your disposal. If you are going to continue sightseeing, stay on Bus 202 for five more stops (to Higashiyama-Shichijō) to explore the southern part of Higashiyama, starting with the temple of **SANJŪSANGEN-DŌ** ⑯. If you have taken Bus 206, stay on it for one more stop (it makes a right turn onto Shichijō-dōri and heads for the station) and get off at the Sanjūsangen-dō-mae bus stop. To start exploring here, take Bus 206 or 208 from Kyōto Eki to the Sanjūsangen-dō-mae stop.

From the Sanjūsangen-dō-mae stop, the temple is to the south just beyond the Kyōto Park Hotel. If you get off Bus 202 at the Higashiyama-Shichijō stop, walk west down Shichijō-dōri and take the first major street to the left. If you plan to see Chishaku-in, go there first. It will allow you to avoid doubling back.

From Sanjūsangen-dō retrace your steps back to Shichijō-dōri and take a right. **CHISHAKU-IN** ⑰, famous for its paintings, will be facing you on the other side of Higashi-ōji-dōri. Back across Higashi-ōji-dōri is the prestigious **KOKURITSU HAKUBUTSUKAN** ⑱. Just north, less than a five-minute walk along Higashi-ōji-dōri of Kokuritsu, is the **KAWAI KANJIRŌ KINENKAN** ⑲, which houses the works of renowned potter Kanjirō Kawai. The next place to visit is a very special temple, **KIYOMIZU-DERA** ⑳. To get there from the museum, cross the major avenue Gojō-dōri and walk north along Higashi-ōji-dōri. The street to the right, Gojō-zaka, leads into Kiyomizu-zaka, which you'll take to the temple.

If you take a right halfway down the road (Kiyomizu-zaka) leading from Kiyomizu-dera, you can walk along the Sannen-zaka and Ninen-zaka (slopes). Take a left after Ninen-zaka and then an immediate right, and continue walking north. After another five minutes you will see, on the right, **KŌDAI-JI** ㉑, a sedate nunnery founded in the early 17th century. Keep heading north; by doing a right–left zigzag at the Maruyama Music Hall, you'll get to **MARUYAMA KŌEN** ㉒. The road to the right (east) leads up the mountainside to **CHŌRAKU-JI** ㉓, a temple famous today for the stone lanterns that lead to it. Proceed north through Maruyama Kōen, and you'll find **CHION-IN** ㉔, headquarters of the Jōdo sect of Buddhism. More paintings by the Kanō school are on view at **SHŌREN-IN** ㉕, a five-minute walk north of Chion-in.

If you missed visiting the Kindai Bijutsukan, Kyōto-shi Bijutsukan, Heian Jingū described in the first part of this tour, note that these are just 10 minutes north of Shōren-in on foot, on the other side of Sanjō-dōri. If you turn right (east) from Shōren-in on Sanjō-dōri, you'll eventually reach the Miyako Hotel; left (west) on Sanjō-dōri leads across Higashi-ōji-dōri to the downtown area and the covered mall. If you turn left on Higashi-ōji-dōri, you will reach Shijō-dōri and the **Gion** district, where geisha live and work.

At the Gion bus stop, Shijō-dōri goes off to the west. Before going down this street, consider taking a short walk east (back into Maruyama Kōen) to **YASAKA JINJA** ㉖, a shrine that is said to bring good health and wealth. Walk back from Yasaka Jinja, cross Higashi-ōji-dōri, and you are in Gion, on Shijō-dōri. On the right-hand corner is the **KYŌTO CRAFT CENTER** ㉗.

Parallel to Shijō-dōri and to the north is Shinmonzen-dōri, a great place to do a little shopping and browsing. Shijō-dōri itself has interesting, less expensive items.

Off Shijō-dōri, halfway between Higashi-ōji-dōri and the Kamogawa, is Hanami-kōji-dōri. The section of this street that runs south of Shijō-dōri (on the right, if you are walking back from the river) will bring you into the heart of the Gion district and the **GION KABURENJŌ THEATER** ㉘.

If you continue west on Shijō-dōri, you'll cross over the Kamogawa. Pontochō-dōri is on the right. Like Gion, this area is known for its nightlife and geisha entertainment. At the north end of Pontochō-dōri, the **PONTO-CHŌ KABURENJŌ THEATER** ㉙ puts on geisha performances.

TIMING
This route is extensive, and it would, if you dutifully covered everything along it, require at least two days. You do need to be selective, especially because you might want to spend 40 minutes or more at such places as Ginkaku-ji, Sanjūsangen-dō, the Kokuritsu Hakubutsukan, and Kiyomizu-dera.

What to See

★ ㉔ **CHION-IN.** The entrance to the temple is through the 79-ft, two-story San-mon. In many people's minds, this is the most daunting temple gate in all of Japan, and it leads to one of Japan's largest temples, the very headquarters of the Jōdo sect of Buddhism, the second-largest Buddhist sect in Japan. The temple has won this distinction because it's the site on which Hōnen, the founder of the Jōdo sect, chose to take his leave of this world by fasting to death in 1212. Chion-in was built in 1234. Because of fires and earthquakes, the oldest standing buildings are the Hon-dō (Main Hall, 1633) and the Daihōjō (Abbots' Quarters, 1639). The temple's belfry houses the largest bell in Japan, which was cast in 1633 and requires 17 monks to ring. The corridor behind the Main Hall, which leads to the Assembly Hall, is an *uguisu-bari* (nightingale floor). This type of floor is constructed to "sing" at every footstep to warn the monks of intruders. Walk underneath the corridor to examine the way the boards and nails are placed to create this inventive burglar alarm. From Kyōto Eki take Bus 206 to the Gion stop. The temple is north of Maruyama Kōen. *400 Hayashi-shita-chō 3-chōme, Yamato-ōji, Higashi-hairu, Shimbashi-dōri, Higashiyama-ku. ¥400. Mar.–Oct., daily 9–4:30; Nov.–Feb., daily 9–4; not all buildings open to public.*

★ ⑰ **CHISHAKU-IN.** The major reason for visiting this temple is for its famous paintings, which were executed by Tōhaku Hasegawa and his son Kyūzo—known as the Hasegawa school, rivals of the Kanō school—and are some of the best examples of Momoyama-period art. These paintings were originally created for the sliding screens at Shōun-in, a temple built in 1591 on the same site but no longer in existence. Shōun-in was commissioned by Hideyoshi Toyotomi. When his concubine, Yodogimi, bore him a son in 1589, Hideyoshi named him Tsurumatsu (crane pine), two symbols of longevity. But the child died at age two, and Shōun-in was built for Tsurumatsu's enshrinement. The Hasegawas were commissioned to make the paintings, which were saved from the fires that destroyed Shōun-in and are now on display in the Exhibition Hall of Chishaku-in. Rich in detail and using strong colors on a gold background, they splendidly display the seasons by using the symbols of cherry, maple, pine, and plum trees and autumn grasses.

You may also want to take a few moments in the pond-viewing garden. It has only a vestige of its former glory, but from the temple's veranda you'll have a pleasing view of the pond and garden. From Kyōto Eki take Bus 206 or 208 to the Higashiyama-

Shichijō stop. Chishaku-in is on the east side of Higashi-ōji-dōri. ¥350. Daily 9–4:30.

★ ㉓ **CHŌRAKU-JI.** Mostly it is the procession of stone lanterns along the path that gives this temple a modest fame. Although it's a pleasant temple, it may not be worth the hard climb up the mountainside. Chōraku-ji is east of Maruyama Kōen. ¥400. Daily 9–5.

⑬ **DENTŌ SANGYŌ KAIKAN** (Kyōto Museum of Traditional Crafts). This museum displays a wide array of traditional Kyōto crafts, hosts educational crafts-making demonstrations, and even has a shop where you can pick up crafts souvenirs. In the basement is a model interior of a traditional town house. From the Dōbutsu-en-mae bus stop, head down the street that leads to Heian Jingū. The museum is inside the torii on your left after the Kindai Bijutsukan. 9–2 Seishōji-chō, Okazaki, Sakyō-ku, tel. 075/761–3421. Free. Tues.–Sun. 9–5 (last entry at 4:30).

 ⑩ **DŌBUTSU-EN** (Kyōto Zoo). The prime reason to stop at the zoo is to entertain your children, if you have any in tow. The zoo has a Children's Corner, where your youngsters can feed the farm animals. It's across from the Dōbutsu-en-mae bus stop. Hoshōji-chō, Okazaki, Sakyō-ku, tel. 075/771–0210. ¥500. Tues.–Sun. 9–5 (winter 9–4:30); when Mon. is national holiday, zoo stays open Mon. and closes Tues.

★ ④ **EIKAN-DŌ.** Officially this temple, founded in 855 by Priest Shinshō, is named Zenrin-ji, but it honors the memory of an 11th-century priest, Priest Eikan, and has popularly come to be known as Eikan-dō. He was a man of the people, and he would lead them in a dance in celebration of Amida Buddha. According to tradition, the Amida statue came to life on one occasion and stepped down from his pedestal to join the dancers. Taken aback, Eikan slowed his dancing feet. Amida looked back over his shoulder to reprimand Eikan for slowing his pace. This legend explains why the unusual statue in the Amida-dō has its face turned to the side, as if glancing backward. A climb to the top of the pagoda affords superb views of the grounds below and Kyōto beyond. With colorful maple trees, the grounds are magnificent in autumn. The buildings here are 16th-century reconstructions made after the originals were destroyed in the Ōnin Civil War (1467–77). Eikan-dō is a 15-minute walk south of Hōnen-in on the Path of Philosophy. ¥500. Daily 9–5 (last entry at 4:30).

★ ❶ **GINKAKU-JI.** Ginkaku-ji means "Temple of the Silver Pavilion," but the temple is not silver; it was only intended to be. Shōgun Yoshimasa Ashikaga (1435–90) commissioned this villa for his retirement. He started it as early as the 1460s, but it was not until 1474 that, disillusioned with politics, he gave his full attention to the construction of his villa and to romance, moon gazing, and the tea ceremony, which he helped develop into a high art. Though he never had time to complete the coating of the pavilion with silver foil, he constructed a dozen or so buildings. Many were designed for cultural pursuits, such as incense and tea ceremonies. At his death, the villa was converted into a Buddhist temple, as was often the custom during the feudal era. However, with the decline of the Ashikaga family, Ginkaku-ji fell into disrepair, and many buildings were destroyed.

All that remain today of the original buildings are Tōgu-dō (East Request Hall) and Ginkaku-ji itself. The four other structures on the grounds were built in the 17th and 19th centuries. The front room of Tōgu-dō is where Yoshimasa is thought to have lived, and the statue of the priest is probably of Yoshimasa himself. The back room, called Dojin-sai (Comradely Abstinence), became the prototype for traditional tea-ceremony rooms.

Ginkaku-ji is a simple and unadorned two-story building. Its appeal lies in the serene exterior shape, which combines Chinese elements with the developing Japanese Muro-machi (1333–1568) architecture. The upper floor contains a gilt image of Kannon (goddess of mercy) said to have been carved by

Unkei, a famous Kamakura-period sculptor; it's not, however, ordinarily open to public view.

★ Ginkaku-ji overlooks the complex **gardens,** attributed to artist and architect Soami (1465–1523), which consist of two contrasting garden sections that together create a balanced, harmonious result. Adjacent to the pavilion is a pond garden, with a composition of rocks and plants designed to afford different perspectives from each viewpoint. The other garden has two sculpted mounds of sand, the higher one symbolizing, perhaps, Mt. Fuji. The garden sparkles in the moonlight and has been aptly named Sea of Silver Sand. The composition of the approach to the garden is also quite remarkable.

To reach Ginkaku-ji, take Bus 5 from Kyōto Eki to the Ginkaku-ji-michi bus stop. Walk on the street along the canal, going east. Cross a north–south canal and Hakusha Son-sō Garden on your right; then continue straight and Ginkaku ji will be in front of you. *Ginkaku-ji-chō, Sakyō-ku. ¥500. Mid-Mar.–Nov., daily 8:30–5; Dec.–mid-Mar., daily 9–4:30.*

★ **GION** (ghee-*own*). Arguably Kyōto's most interesting neighborhood, this is the legendary haunt of geisha. In the evening, amid the glow of teahouse and restaurant lanterns, you can see them scurrying about, white faced, on the way to their appointments. In their wake their *maiko* follow—the young apprentice geisha whom you can identify by the longer sleeves of their kimonos. On a level equal to the world of temples and gardens, Gion is the place for gaijin to fantasize about Japan's fabled floating world.

The heart of the district is on Hanami-kōji-dōri. Heading north, the street intersects with Shinmonzen-dōri, which is famous for its antiques shops and art galleries. Here you'll find collectors' items—at collectors' prices—which make for interesting browsing, if not buying. The shops on Shijō-dōri, which parallels Shinmonzen-dōri to the south, carry slightly more affordable items of the geisha world, from handcrafted hair ornaments to incense to parasols.

★ ㉘ **GION KABURENJŌ THEATER.** Because Westerners have little opportunity to enjoy a geisha's performance in a private party setting—which would require a proper recommendation of, and probably the presence of, a geisha's respected client—a popular entertainment during the month of April is the Miyako Odori (Cherry-Blossom Dance), presented at this theater. During the musical presentations, geisha wear their elaborate traditional kimonos and makeup. Next door to the theater is **Gion Corner**, where demonstrations of traditional performing arts take place nightly March–November. *Gion Hanami-kōji, Higashiyama-ku, tel. 075/561–1115.*

HAKUSHA SON-SŌ GARDEN. The modest villa of the late painter Hashimoto Kansetsu has an exquisite stone garden and teahouse open to the public. To get here, take Bus 5 from Kyōto Eki to the Ginkaku-ji-michi stop. Walk east on the street along the canal. Just after the street crosses another canal flowing north–south, Hakusha Son-sō will be on the right. *¥800; with tea and sweets, an extra ¥800. Daily 10–5 (last entry at 4:30).*

★ ⑭ **HEIAN JINGŪ.** One of the city's newest historical sites, Heian Jingū was built in 1894 to mark the 1,100th anniversary of the founding of Kyōto. The shrine honors two emperors: Kammu (737–806), who founded the city in 794, and Kōmei (1831–66), the last emperor to live out his reign in Kyōto. The new buildings are for the most part replicas of the old Imperial Palace, at two-thirds the original size. In fact, because the original palace (rebuilt many times) was finally destroyed in 1227, and only scattered pieces of information exist relating to its construction, Heian Jingū should be taken as a Meiji interpretation of the old palace. Still, the dignity and the relative spacing of the **East Hon-den** and **West Hon-den** (the Main Halls), and the **Daigoku-den** (Great Hall of State), in which the Heian emperor would issue decrees, conjure up an image of how magnificent the Heian court must have been. During New Year's, kimono-clad and gray-suited Japanese come to pay homage, trampling over the imposing gravel forecourt leading to Daigoku-den.

There are three stroll gardens at Heian Jingū positioned east, west, and north of the shrine itself. They follow the Heian aesthetic of focusing on a large pond, a rare feature at a Shintō shrine. Another notable element is the stepping-stone path that crosses the water—its steps are recycled pillars from a 16th-century bridge that spanned the Kamo-gawa before an earthquake destroyed it.

Spring, with sakura in full bloom, is a superb time to visit. An even better time to see the shrine is during the Jidai Festival, held on October 22, which celebrates the founding of Kyōto. The pageant, a procession of 2,000 people attired in costumes from every period of Kyōto history, winds its way from the original site of the Imperial Palace and ends at the Heian Jingū.

Another choice time to come to the shrine is on June 1–2 for **Takigi Nō performances,** so named because they are held at night, in open air, lighted by takigi (burning firewood). Performances take place on a stage built before the shrine's Daigoku-den.

From the Dōbutsu-en-mae bus stop, follow the street between the Kyōto-shi Bijutsukan and the Kindai Bijutsukan directly to the shrine. Okazakinishi Tennō-chō, Sakyō-ku. Garden ¥600; Takigi Nō ¥3,300 at the gate, ¥2,500 in advance. Call Tourist Information Center for advance tickets: 075/371–5649. Mid-Mar.–Aug., daily 8:30–5:30; Sept.–Oct. and early Mar., daily 8:30–5; Nov.–Feb., daily 8:30–4:30.

★ ❸ **HŌNEN-IN.** The walk through the trees leading to the temple is mercifully quiet and comforting, but not many people come to this humble, thatched-roof structure. The temple was built in 1680, on a site that in the 13th century simply consisted of an open-air

Amida Buddha statue. Hōnen-in honors Priest Hōnen (1133–1212), the founder of the Jōdo sect, who brought Buddhism down from its lofty peak to the common folk by making the radical claim that all were equal in the eyes of Buddha. Hōnen focused on faith in the Amida Nyorai; he believed that *nembutsu*—"Namu Amida Butsu," the invocation of Amida Buddha—which he is said to have repeated up to 60,000 times a day, and reliance on Amida, the "all-merciful," were the path to salvation. His ideas threatened other sects, especially the Tendai. The established Buddhist powers pressured then-emperor Gotoba to diminish Hōnen's influence over the masses. At about the same time, two of the emperor's concubines became nuns after hearing some of Hōnen's disciples preaching. The incident provided Gotoba with an excuse to decry the Jōdo sect as immoral, with the charge that its priests were seducing noblewomen. Emperor Gotoba had Anraku and Juren, two of Hōnen's disciples, publicly executed and Hōnen sent into exile. Eventually, in 1211, Hōnen was pardoned and permitted to return to Kyōto, where a year later, at Chion-in, he fasted to death at the age of 79. From the Path of Philosophy, at the first large bridge as you walk south, turn off the path and take the road east. *Free. Daily 7–4.*

⑲ **KAWAI KANJIRŌ KINENKAN** (Kawai Kanjirō Memorial House). Taking his inspiration from a traditional rural Japanese cottage, Kanjirō Kawai, one of Japan's most renowned potters, designed and lived in this house, now a museum. He was one of the leaders of the Mingei (folk art) movement, which sought to revive interest in traditional folk arts during the 1920s and '30s, when all things Western were in vogue in Japan. On display are some of the artist's personal memorabilia and, of more interest, some of his exquisite works. An admirer of Western, Chinese, and Korean ceramics techniques, Kawai won many awards, including the Grand Prix at the 1937 Paris World Exposition. From Kyōto Eki take Bus 206 or 208 to the Sanjūsangen-dō-mae stop and then head east to the end of Shichijō-dōri. The house is a five-minute walk north along Higashi-ōji-dōri. *Gojō-zaka, Higashiyama-ku, tel. 075/*

561–3585. ¥900. Tues.–Sun. 10–5; when Mon. is national holiday, museum stays open Mon. and closes Tues. Closed Aug. 10–20 and Dec. 24–Jan. 7.

⑫ **KINDAI BIJUTSUKAN** (National Museum of Modern Art). The museum is known for its collection of 20th-century Japanese paintings and its ceramic treasures by Kanjirō Kawai, Rosanjin Kitaōji, Shōji Hamada, and others. Established in 1903, it reopened in 1986 in a building designed by Fumihiko Maki, one of the top contemporary architects in Japan. From the Dōbutsu-en-mae bus stop, walk down the street that leads to the Heian Jingū. The museum is on the left inside the torii, Enshōji-chō, Okazaki, Sakyō-ku, tel. 075/761–4111. ¥420; additional fee for special exhibitions. Tues.–Sun. 9:30–5.

★ ⑳ **KIYOMIZU-DERA.** Unique Kiyomizu-dera, one of the most visited temples in Kyōto and a prominent feature in the city's skyline, stands out because it is built into a steep hillside, with 139 giant pillars supporting part of its main hall. In the past people would come here to escape the open political intrigue of Kyōto and to scheme in secrecy.

The temple's location is marvelous—one reason for coming here is the view. From the wooden veranda, one of the few temple verandas where you can walk around without removing your shoes, there are fine views of the city and a breathtaking look at the valley below. "Have you the courage to jump from the veranda of Kiyomizu?" is a saying asked when someone sets out on a daring new venture.

Interestingly enough, Kiyomizu-dera does not belong to one of the local Kyōto Buddhist sects but rather to the Hossō sect, which developed in Nara. The temple honors the popular 11-faced Kannon (goddess of mercy), who can bring about easy childbirth. Over time Kiyomizu-dera has become "everyone's temple." You'll see evidence of this throughout the grounds, from the little Jizō Bosatsu statues (representing the god of travel and children) stacked in rows to the many *koma-inu* (mythical guard dogs) marking the pathways, which have been donated by the temple's grateful patrons. The original Kiyomizu-dera was built here in 798, four years after Kyōto was founded; the current structure dates from 1633.

Shops selling souvenirs, religious articles, and ceramics line Kiyomizu-zaka, the street leading to the temple. There are also tea shops where you can sample *yatsuhashi*—doughy, triangular sweets filled with cinnamon-flavor bean paste—a Kyōto specialty. Because of the immense popularity of the temple on the hill above it, this narrow slope is often crowded with sightseers and bus tour groups, but the magnificent temple is worth the struggle. From Kyōto Eki take Bus 206 to the Kiyomizu-michi stop. From Kawai Kanjirō Kinenkan cross the major avenue, Gojō-dōri, and walk up Higashi-ōji-dōri. The street to the right, Gojō-zaka, leads into Kiyomizu-zaka, which you'll take to the temple. *Kiyomizu 1-chōme, Higashiyama-ku. ¥300. Daily 6–6.*

NEED A BREAK? **Kasagi-ya** has been serving tea at the foot of Kiyomizu-dera for more than a century. Step inside, and you'll feel as if you've been whisked back in time. Order the *o-hagi* (sweet bean and rice dumplings); they'll complement the bitterness of your tea and give you a sugar rush for your final assault on the temples. *349 Masuya-chō, Kōdai-ji, Higashiyama-ku, tel. 075/561–9562. Closed Tues. No dinner.*

★ ㉑ **KŌDAI-JI.** This quiet nunnery established in the early 17th century provides a tranquil alternative to the crowds of nearby Kiyomizu-dera. The temple was built as a memorial to Hideyoshi Toyotomi by his wife, Kita-no-Mandokoro, who lived out her remaining days in the nunnery here. The famous 17th-century landscaper Kobori Enshū designed the gardens, and artists of the Tosa school decorated the ceilings of the Kaisan-dō (Founder's Hall) with raised lacquer and paintings. The teahouse above on the hill, designed by tea master Sen-no-Rikyū, has a unique umbrella-shape bamboo ceiling and a thatched roof. From Kyōto Eki take Bus 206 to the Higashiyama-yasui bus stop. ¥500. Apr.–Nov., daily 9–4:30; Dec.– Mar., daily 9–4.

⑱ KOKURITSU HAKUBUTSUKAN (Kyōto National Museum). Exhibitions at this prestigious museum change regularly, but you can count on an excellent display of paintings, sculpture, textiles, calligraphy, ceramics, lacquerware, metalwork, and archaeological artifacts from its permanent collection of more than 8,000 works of art. From Kyōto Eki take Bus 206 or 208 to the Sanjūsangen-dō-mae stop. The museum is across Higashi-ōji-dōri from Chishaku-in. Yamato-oji-dōri, Higashiyama-ku, tel. 075/ 541–1151. ¥420; additional fee for special exhibitions. Tues.–Sun. 9–4:30.

★ **⑦ KONCHI-IN.** The two gardens of this shrine especially merit a visit: famous tea master and landscape designer Kobori Enshū completed them in 1632, under commission by Zen priest Sūden in accordance with the will of Ieyasu Tokugawa. One has a pond in the shape of the Chinese character kokoro (heart). The other is a dry garden with a gravel area in the shape of a boat, a large flat worshiping stone, and a backdrop of o-karikomi (tightly pruned shrubbery). The two rock groupings in front of a plant-filled mound are in the crane-and-tortoise style. Since ancient times these creatures have been associated with longevity, beauty, and eternal youth. In the feudal eras the symbolism of the crane and the tortoise became very popular with the samurai class, whose profession often left them with only the hope of immortality. Though not on the same grounds as ☞ **Nanzen-ji,** this temple is in fact part of the Nanzen-ji complex. To get here, leave Nanzen-ji and take the side street to the left. 86 Fukuchi-chō, Nanzen-ji, Sakyō-ku. ¥400. Mar.–Nov., daily 8:30–5; Dec.– Feb., daily 8:30–4:30.

㉗ KYŌTO CRAFT CENTER. Kyōto residents know to come to this collection of stores to shop for fine contemporary and traditional crafts—ceramics, lacquerware, prints, and textiles. You can also purchase moderately priced souvenirs, such as dolls, coasters, bookmarks, and paper products. From Kyōto Eki take Bus 206 to the Gion stop. The center is on the corner of Shijō-dōri and Higashi-ōji-dōri. *Shijō-dōri, Gion-machi, Higashiyama-ku, tel. 075/561–9660. Thurs.–Tues. 11–7.*

⑮ KYŌTO HANDICRAFT CENTER. Seven floors of everything Japanese, from dolls to cassette recorders, is on sale. The center caters to tourists with its English-speaking staff. It's a good place to browse, even if you end up deciding that the prices are too high. From the Gion bus stop take Bus 202 or 206 five stops north on Higashi-ōji-dōri to the Kumano Jinja-mae bus stop. From Kyōto Eki use Bus 206; the center is across Maruta-machi-dōri from the Heian Jingū. *Kumano Jinja Higashi, Sakyō-ku, tel. 075/761–5080. Mar.–Nov., daily 9:30–6; Dec.–Feb., daily 9:30–5:30.*

⑧ KYŌTO INTERNATIONAL COMMUNITY HOUSE. Set on expansive grounds, the center has library and information facilities and rental halls for public performances. The bulletin board by the entryway is full of tips on housing opportunities, study, and events in Kyōto. The KICH also offers weekly lessons in tea ceremony, *koto* (a 13-stringed instrument), calligraphy, and Japanese language at reasonable prices. The book *Easy Living in Kyōto* (available free) gives helpful information for longer stays. The Community House is off the intersection at the foot of the road to Nanzen-ji. *2–1 Torii-chō, Awata-guchi, Sakyō-ku, tel. 075/752–3010. Free. Tues.–Sun. 9–9; when Mon. is national holiday, Community House stays open Mon. and closes Tues..*

⑪ KYŌTO-SHI BIJUTSUKAN (Kyōto Municipal Museum of Art). This space serves mostly as a gallery for traveling shows and local art-society exhibits. It owns a collection of Japanese paintings of the Kyōto school, a selection of which goes on display once a year. From the Dōbutsu-en-mae bus stop, walk down the street that leads to the Heian Jingū. The museum is on the right inside the torii. *Enshōji-chō, Okazaki, Sakyō-ku, tel. 075/771–4107. Approximately*

¥1,000, depending upon exhibition. Tues.–Sun. 9–5 (last entry at 4:30); when Mon. is national holiday, the museum stays open Mon. and closes Tues.

㉒ MARUYAMA KŌEN. You can rest your weary feet at this small park, home to the Maruyama Music Hall. A few wandering vendors are usually around to supply refreshment. From Kyōto Eki take Bus 206 to the Higashiyama stop; the park is north of Kōdai-ji.

❾ MURIN-AN GARDEN. The property was once part of Nanzen-ji, but in 1895 it was sold to Prince Yamagata, a former prime minister and advocate of the reforms that followed the Meiji Restoration. Unlike more traditional Japanese gardens, which adopt a more restrained sense of harmony, Murin-an allows more freedom of movement. This is right in step with the Westernizing that the Meiji Restoration brought upon Japan. The garden is south of the Dōbutsu-en-mae bus stop. Enter from the side road on the other side of a canal. ¥350. Daily 9–4:30.

★ **❻ NANZEN-JI.** Like the nearby temple of Ginkaku-ji, this former aristocratic retirement villa was turned into a temple on the death of its owner, Emperor Kameyama (1249–1305). The 15th-century Ōnin Civil War demolished the buildings, but some were resurrected during the 16th century. Nanzen-ji has become one of Kyōto's most important temples, in part because it is the headquarters of the Rinzai sect of Zen Buddhism. You enter the temple through the 1628 **San-mon** (Triple Gate), the classic "gateless" gate of Zen Buddhism that symbolizes entrance into the most sacred part of the temple precincts. From the top floor of the gate you can view Kyōto spread out below. Whether or not you ascend the steep steps, pause a moment at the statue of Goemon Ishikawa, a Robin Hood–style outlaw of Japan who hid in this gate until his capture.

On through the gate is **Hōjō** (Abbots' Quarters), a National Treasure. Inside, screens with impressive 16th-century paintings divide the chambers. These wall panels of the *Twenty-Four*

Paragons of Filial Piety and Hermits were created by Eitoku Kanō (1543–90) of the Kanō school—in effect the Kanō family, because the school consists of eight generations of one bloodline, Eitoku being from the fifth. Kobori Enshū created the Zen-style garden, commonly called the Leaping Tiger Garden and an excellent example of the karesansui style, attached to the Hōjō. Unusual here, the large rocks are grouped with clipped azaleas, maples, pines, and moss, all positioned against a plain white well behind the raked gravel expanse. The greenery serves to connect the garden quite effectively with the lush forested hillside beyond.

Within Nanzen-ji's 27 pine-tree-covered acres sit several other temples, known more for their gardens than for their buildings. One worth visiting if you have time is **Nanzen-in,** once the temporary abode of Emperor Kameyama. Nanzen-in has a mausoleum and a garden that dates from the 14th century; a small creek passes through it. Nanzen-in is not as famous as other temples, making it a peaceful place to visit. From Nomura Bijutsukan, walk south along the main path to Nanzen-ji; the temple complex will be on your left. *Main temple building ¥400, San-mon or Nanzen-in ¥200. Mar.–Nov., daily 8:40–5; Dec.–Feb., daily 8:40–4:30.*

⑤ **NOMURA BIJUTSUKAN.** Instead of bequeathing their villas to Buddhist sects, the modern wealthy Japanese tend to donate their art collections to museums, as was the case here. Tokushichi Nomura, founder of the Daiwa Bank and a host of other companies, donated his collection of scrolls, paintings, tea-ceremony utensils, ceramics, and other art objects to establish his namesake museum. The museum is south of Eikan-dō on the west side of the street. *61 Shimogawara-chō, Nanzen-ji, Sakyō-ku, tel. 075/751–0374. ¥700. Late Mar.–mid-June and mid-Sept.–early Dec., Tues.–Sun. 10–4:30 (last entry at 4).*

② **PATH OF PHILOSOPHY.** Cherry trees, which are spectacular in bloom, line this walkway along the canal, known in Japanese as

Tetsugaku-no-michi. It has traditionally been a place for contemplative strolls since a famous scholar, Ikutaro Nishida (1870–1945), took his constitutional here. Now professors and students have to push their way through tourists who take the same stroll and whose interests lie mainly with the path's specialty shops. Along the path are several coffee shops and small restaurants. Omen, one block west of the Path of Philosophy, is an inexpensive, popular restaurant, known for its homemade white noodles.

From Kyōto Eki take Bus 5 to the Ginkaku-ji-michi bus stop. Walk east on the street that follows the canal. Just after the street crosses a north–south canal, the path begins on your right.

㉙ PONTO-CHŌ KABURENJŌ THEATER. Like Gion, Ponto-chō is known for its nightlife and geisha entertainment. At the north end of Pontochō-dōri, the Ponto-chō Kaburenjō presents geisha song-and-dance performances in the spring (May 1–24) and autumn (October 15–November 7). The theater sits on the west side of the Kamo-gawa between Sanjō and Shijō streets. *Ponto-chō, Sanjō-sagaru, Nakagyō-ku, tel. 075/221–2025.*

★ **⑯ SANJŪSANGEN-DŌ.** Everyone knows this temple as Sanjūsangen-dō even though it's officially called Rengeō-in. *Sanjūsan* means "33," which is the number of spaces between the 35 pillars that lead down the narrow, 394-ft-long hall of the temple. Enthroned in the middle of the hall is the 6-ft-tall, 1,000-handed Kannon—a National Treasure—carved by Tankei, a sculptor of the Kamakura period (1192–1333). One thousand smaller statues of Kannon surround the large statue, and in the corridor behind are the 28 guardian deities who protect the Buddhist universe. Notice the frivolous-faced Garuda, a bird that feeds on dragons. Are you wondering about the 33 spaces mentioned earlier? Kannon can assume 33 different shapes on her missions of mercy. Because there are 1,001 statues of Kannon in the hall, 33,033 shapes are possible. People come to the hall to see if they can find the likeness of a loved one (a deceased relative) among the many statues.

From Kyōto Eki take Bus 206, 208, or 100 to the Sanjūsangen-dō-mae stop. The temple will be to the south, just beyond the Kyōto Park Hotel. 657 Sanjūsangen-dō Mawari-chō, Higashiyama-ku. ¥600. Apr.–mid-Nov., daily 8–5; mid-Nov.–Mar., daily 9–4.

Sannen-zaka and Ninen-zaka (Sannen and Ninen slopes). With their cobbled paths and delightful wooden buildings, these two lovely winding streets are fine examples of old Kyōto. This area is one of four historic preservation districts in Kyōto, and the shops along the way sell local crafts and wares such as Kiyomizu-yaki (Kiyomizu-style pottery), Kyōto dolls, bamboo basketry, rice crackers, and antiques. From Kiyomizu-dera turn right halfway down the Kiyomizu-zaka.

★ ㉕ **SHŌREN-IN.** Paintings by the Kanō school are on view at this temple, a five-minute walk north of Chion-in. Though the temple's present building dates only from 1895, the sliding screens of the Hon-dō (Main Hall) have the works of Motonobu Kanō, second-generation Kanō, and Mitsunobu Kanō of the sixth generation. In the pleasant garden an immense camphor tree sits at the entrance gate, and azaleas surround a balanced grouping of rocks and plants. The garden was no doubt more grandiose when artist and architect Soami designed it in the 16th century, but with the addition of paths through the garden, it's a pleasant place to stroll. Another garden on the east side of the temple is sometimes attributed, probably incorrectly, to Kobori Enshū. Occasionally, koto concerts are held in the evening in the Soami Garden (for concert schedules check with a Japan Travel Bureau office tel. 075/361–7241). From Kyōto Eki take Bus 206 to the Higashiyama-Sanjō stop. ¥500. Daily 9–5.

★ ㉖ **YASAKA JINJA.** Your business and health problems might come to a resolution at this Shintō shrine—leave a message for the god of prosperity and good health, to whom Yasaka Jinja is dedicated. Because it's close to the shopping districts, worshipers drop by for quick salvation. Especially at New Year's, Kyōto residents flock here to ask for good fortune in the coming year. From Kyōto Eki take Bus 206 or 100 to the Gion bus stop; the shrine is just off Higashi-ōji-dōri. 625 Gion-machi, Kitagawa, Higashiyama-ku. Free. 24 hrs.

WESTERN KYŌTO

This tour of western Kyōto begins with the major northern sights, Kitano Tenman-gu first of all. If you're short on time, start instead at Daitoku-ji. As in eastern Kyōto, the city's western precincts are filled with remarkable religious architecture, in particular the eye-popping golden Kinkaku-ji and Kitano Tenman-gū, with its monthly flea market.

Numbers in the text correspond to numbers in the margin and on the Western Kyōto and Arashiyama map.

A Good Tour

Start with the Shintō **KITANO TENMAN-GŪ** ㉚, where a flea market is held on the 25th of each month. About a five-minute walk north of Kitano is **HIRANO JINJA** ㉛, a shrine with wonderful cherry trees in its garden. After visiting the shrine, head for **DAITOKU-JI** ㉜, a large 24-temple complex. To get here from Hirano Jinja head east to the bus stop at the intersection of Sembon-dōri and Imadegawa-dōri. Climb on Bus 206 and take it north for about 10 minutes. Be sure to see the subtemple, **DAISEN-IN** ㉝, well known for its landscape paintings and for its karesansui garden. Other subtemples to visit if you have time are Kōtō-in and Ryogen-in. To get to the next stop, the impressive **KINKAKU-JI** ㉞, hop on Bus 12 west on Kita-ōji-dōri for a 10-minute ride to the Kinkaku-ji-mae stop.

From Kinkaku-ji walk back to the Kinkaku-ji-mae bus stop and take Bus 12 or 59 south for 10 minutes to the Ritsumeikan-daigaku-mae stop. The nearby **DŌMOTO INSHŌ BIJUTSUKAN** ㉟ exhibits works by the 20th-century abstract artist Inshō Dōmoto.

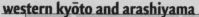

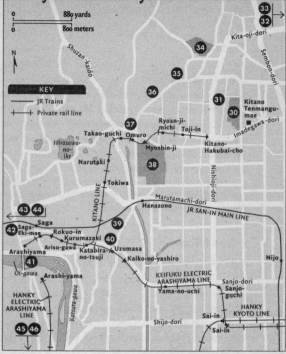

0 | 880 yards
0 | 800 meters

N

Kita-oji-dori

Shuzan kaido

Sembon-dori

34

35

36

31 · Kitano
Tenmangu-
mae

30

KEY
— JR Trains
+ Private rail line

Ryoan-ji-
michi   Toji-in
37 Omuro

Takao-guchi

Kitano-
Hakubai-cho

Hirosawa-
no-ike

Myoshin-ji

Imadegawa-dori

Narutaki

38

Nishioji-dori

Tokiwa

KITANO LINE

Marutamachi-dori

Hanazono

JR SAN-IN MAIN LINE

43 44

Saga

39

Saga-
42 Eki-mae   Rokuo-in
Kurumazaki

Arashiyama Arisu-gawa 40 Uzumasa
41 Katabira- Kaiko-no-yashiro
no-tsuji

Oi-gawa   Arashi-yama

Katsura-gawa

Nijo

KEIFUKU ELECTRIC
ARASHIYAMA LINE

Yama-no-uchi

Sanjo-dori
Sanjo-
guchi

HANKY
ELECTRIC
ARASHIYAMA
LINE

HANKY
KYOTO LINE

Sai-in

45 46

Shijo-dori

Sai-in

Bamboo forest, **43**

Daisen-in, **33**

Daitoku-ji, **32**

Dōmoto Inshō
Bijutsukan, **35**

Hirano Jinja, **31**

Katsura Rikyū
(Katsura Detached
Villa), **46**

Kinkaku-ji, **34**

Kitano
Tenman-gū, **30**

Koinzan
Saihō-ji, **45**

Kōryū-ji, **40**

Myōshin-ji, **38**

Ninna-ji, **37**

Ōkōchi Sansō, **44**

Ryōan-ji, **36**

Tenryū-ji, **42**

Togetsu-kyō-
bashi, **41**

Uzumasa Eiga
Mura, **39**

When you leave the museum, either get on Bus 12 or 59 or walk for about 10 minutes south; **RYŌAN-JI** ㊱ will be on your right.

From Ryōan-ji it's about 1½ km (1 mi) farther south on Bus 26 to Myōshin-ji. En route you'll pass **NINNA-JI** ㊲ on the right, a temple that was once the palace of Emperor Omuro. From Ninna-ji, take the street veering to the left (southwest); within ¾ km (½ mi) you'll reach **MYŌSHIN-JI** ㊳. Another option from Ryōan-ji is to take Bus 12 or 59 three stops south to Ninna-ji and then change to Bus 8 or 10 to Myōshin-ji. Here you can see Japan's oldest bell. The other (sub-) temple to visit here is Taizō-in, which contains the painting *Four Sages of Mt. Shang*, by Sanraku Kanō. Leave the temple complex by the south side, and you can pick up Bus 61 or 62; both go southwest to **UZUMASA EIGA MURA** ㊴, Japan's equivalent of Hollywood's Universal Studios. If you have no interest in stopping here—a visit will take at least two or three hours—continue on the bus to **KŌRYŪ-JI** ㊵, a short walk south of Uzumasa Eiga Mura. Kōryū-ji is one of Kyōto's oldest temples, with many famous works of art, including the Miroku Bosatsu.

You're close to the Arashiyama district now and can take the Keifuku Electric Railway Arashiyama Line west to Tenryū-ji Eki and the bamboo forest just to the north for a pleasant end to the day. You may get the chance to watch some cormorant fishing on the Oi-gawa.

If you'd rather head back into central Kyōto, it's easy to do so from Kōryū-ji. Either take the bus (Nos. 60–64) back past the Movie Village to JR Hanazono Eki, where the JR San-in Main Line will take you into Kyōto Eki, or take the privately owned Keifuku Electric Railway Arashiyama Line east to its last stop at Shijō-Ōmiya. This stop is on Shijō-dōri, from which Bus 201 or 203 can take you to Gion; or take Bus 26 to Kyōto Eki.

TIMING

If you're quick, you can cover all these sights in a day. If you don't have a lot of time in Kyōto, it would be better, while you're in western Kyōto, to skip a few sights so that you can make your way to Arashiyama in the afternoon.

What to See

★ 33 **DAISEN-IN.** Of all the subtemples at ☞ **Daitoku-ji,** Daisen-in is perhaps the best known—in part for its excellent landscape paintings by the renowned Soami (1465–1523), as well as its karesansui garden, which some attribute to Soami and others to Kogaku Soko (1465–1548). In the garden, the sand and stone represent the eternal aspects of nature, and the streams suggest the course of life. The single rock, once owned by Shōgun Yoshimasa Ashikaga, may be seen as a ship. Be aware that Daisen-in has its share of commercial accretions. *See* Daitoku-ji, *below,* for directions to Daisen-in. ¥400. *Daily 9–5 (9–4:30 in winter).*

★ 32 **DAITOKU-JI.** The Daitoku-ji complex of the Rinzai sect of Zen Buddhism consists of 24 temples in all, several of which are open to the public. The original temple was founded in 1319 by Priest Daito Kokushi (1282–1337), but fires during the Ōnin Civil War destroyed it in 1468. Most buildings you see today were built under the patronage of Hideyoshi Toyotomi. However, it is thought that Priest Ikkyū oversaw its development. Ikkyū, known for his rather startling juxtapositions of the sacred and the profane—he was a priest and a poet—is reported to have said, "Brothels are more suitable settings for meditation than temples."

The layout of the temple is straightforward. Running from north to south are the Chokushi-mon (Gate of Imperial Messengers), the San-mon (Triple Gate), the Butsu-den (Buddha Hall), the Hattō (Lecture Hall), and the Hōjō (Abbots' Quarters). The 23 subtemples are on the west side of these main buildings and were donated mainly by the wealthy vassals of Toyotomi.

The **Chokushi-mon** originally served as the south gate of Kyōto's Imperial Palace when it was constructed in 1590. Then, Empress Meisho in the mid-17th century bequeathed it to Daitoku-ji. Note the curved-gable style of the gate, typical of the Momoyama period. The **San-mon** is noteworthy for the addition of its third story, designed by tea master Sen-no-Rikyū (1521–91), who is buried in the temple grounds. Three subtemples in the complex are noteworthy: ☞ **Daisen-in,** Kōtō-in, and Ryogen-in.

The subtemple **Kōtō-in** is famous for its long, maple-tree–lined approach and the single stone lantern that is central to the main garden. The fee is ¥400, and the temple stays open from 9 until 4:30 or 5 (enter 30 minutes before closing).

Ryogen-in is not as popular as some of the other temples of Daitoku-ji, but it is often quiet and peaceful. The subtemple has five small gardens of moss and stone, one of which, on the north side, is the oldest in Daitoku-ji. The fee is ¥350, and the temple stays open 9–4:30 (enter 30 minutes before closing).

There are several ways to get to the temple from downtown Kyōto. Take the subway north from Kyōto Eki to Kita-ōji Eki, from which any bus going west along Kita-ōji-dōri will take you to the Daitoku-ji-mae stop. You can also take Bus 12 north up Horikawa-dōri and disembark soon after the bus makes a left on Kita-ōji-dōri. From western Kyōto Bus 204, which runs up Nishi-ōji-dōri, and Bus 206, which runs up Sembon-dōri, will also take you to the temple. *Daitoku-ji-chō, Murasakino, Kita-ku. Admission to different temples varies; the average is ¥500. Daily; temple hrs vary between 9 and 4.*

35 **DŌMOTO INSHŌ BIJUTSUKAN** (Dōmoto Inshō Art Museum). Twentieth-century abstract artist Inshō Dōmoto created the painting and sculpture exhibited here. From the Kinkaku-ji-mae bus stop, take Bus 12 or 59 south for 10 minutes to Ritsumeikan-

Daigaku-mae. *Kami-Yanagi-chō, Hirano, Kita-ku, tel. 075/463–1348. ¥500. Tues.–Sun. 10–5.*

★ **③** **HIRANO JINJA.** This complex of four shrine buildings dates from the 17th century, but its ancestry is ancient. The shrine was brought from Nagaoka—Japan's capital after Nara and before Kyōto—as one of many shrines used to protect the budding new Heian-kyō, as Kyōto was then called, during its formative years. The buildings are less remarkable than the gardens, with their 80 varieties of cherry trees. Take either Bus 50 or 52 from downtown Kyōto or Kyōto Eki. The ride takes a little more than a half hour. The shrine is about a 10-minute walk north of the Kitano Tenman-gū-mae bus stop. *Miyamoto-chō 1, Hirano, Kita-ku. Free. Daily 6–5.*

★ **③** **KINKAKU-JI** (Temple of the Golden Pavilion). For a retirement home, Kinkaku-ji is pretty magnificent. Shōgun Yoshimitsu Ashikaga (1358–1409) had it constructed in 1393 for the time when he would quit politics—the following year, in fact—to manage the affairs of state through the new shōgun, his 10-year-old son. On Yoshimitsu's death, his son followed his father's wishes and converted the villa into a temple named Rokuōn-ji. The structure sits, following the Shinden style of the Heian period, at the edge of the lake. Pillars support the three-story pavilion, which extends over the pond and is reflected in the calm waters. It's a beautiful sight, designed to suggest an existence somewhere between heaven and earth. The pavilion was the shōgun's statement of his prestige and power. To underscore that statement, he had the ceiling of the third floor of the pavilion covered in gold leaf. Not only the harmony and balance of the pavilion and its reflection, but also the richness of color shimmering in the light and in the water, make Kinkaku-ji one of Kyōto's most powerful visions.

In 1950 a student monk with metaphysical aspirations torched Kinkaku-ji, burning it to the ground. (Yukio Mishima's book *Temple of the Golden Pavilion* is a fictional attempt to get into the mind of the student.) Kinkaku-ji was rebuilt in 1955 based on the original design, except that all three stories were covered with gold leaf, in accordance with the shōgun's original intention, instead of only the third-floor ceiling.

Marveling at this pavilion, you might find it difficult to imagine the era in which Shōgun Yoshimitsu Ashikaga lived out his golden years. The country was in turmoil, and Kyōto residents suffered severe famines and plagues—local death tolls sometimes reached 1,000 a day. The temple is a short walk from the Kinkaku-ji-mae bus stop. From Daisen-in the ride on Bus 12 takes about 10 minutes. 1 Kinkaku-ji-chō, Kita-ku. ¥400. Daily 9–5.

★ ③⓪ **KITANO TENMAN-GŪ**. This shrine was originally dedicated to Tenjin, the god of thunder. Then, around 942, Michizane Sugawara was enshrined here. In his day, Michizane was a noted poet and politician—until Emperor Go-daigo ascended to the throne. Michizane was accused of treason and sent to exile on Kyūshū, where he died. For decades thereafter Kyoto suffered inexplicable calamities. The answer came in Go-daigo's dream: Michizane's spirit would not rest until he had been pardoned. Because the dream identified Michizane with the god of thunder, Kitano Tenman-gū was dedicated to him. On top of that, Michizane's political rank was posthumously restored. When that was not enough, he was promoted to a higher position and later to prime minister.

Kitano Tenman-gū was also the place where Hideyoshi Toyotomi held an elaborate tea party, inviting the whole of Kyōto to join him—creating a major opportunity for the local aristocracy to show off its finest tea bowls and related paraphernalia. Apart from unifying the warring clans of Japan and attempting to conquer Korea, Toyotomi is remembered in Kyōto as the man responsible for restoring many of the city's temples and shrines during the late 16th century. The shrine's present structure dates from 1607. A large **market** is held on the grounds on the 25th of each month. There are food stalls, and an array of antiques, old kimonos, and other collectibles are sold. Take either Bus 100 or

50 from Kyōto Eki and get off at Kitano Tenman-gū-mae. The ride takes a little more than a half hour. *Imakoji-agaru, Onmae-dori, Kamigyō-ku. Shrine free, plum garden ¥500 (includes green tea). Shrine Apr.–Oct., daily 5–5; Nov.–Mar, daily 5:30–5:30; plum garden Feb.–Mar., daily 10–4.*

★ **40 KŌRYŪ-JI.** One of Kyōto's oldest temples, Kōryū-ji was founded in 622 by Kawakatsu Hata in memory of Prince Shōtoku (572–621). Shōtoku, known for issuing the Seventeen-Article Constitution, was the first powerful advocate of Buddhism after it was introduced to Japan in 552. In the Hattō (Lecture Hall) of the main temple stand three statues, each a National Treasure. The center of worship is the seated figure of Buddha, flanked by the figures of the Thousand-Handed Kannon and Fukukenjaku-Kannon. In the Taishi-dō (Rear Hall), there is a wooden statue of Prince Shōtoku, which is thought to have been carved by him personally. Another statue of Shōtoku in this hall was probably made when he was 16 years old.

The numerous works of art in Kōryū-ji's Reihō-den (Treasure House) include many National Treasures. The most famous of all is the **Miroku Bosatsu,** Japan's number one National Treasure. This image of Buddha is the epitome of serenity, and of all the Buddhas in Kyōto this is perhaps the most captivating. No one knows when it was made, but it is thought to be from the 6th or 7th century, carved, perhaps, by Shōtoku himself.

From Kyōto Eki take the JR San-in Main Line to Hanazono Eki and then board Bus 61. From Shijō-Ōmiya Eki, in central Kyōto, take the Keifuku Electric Arashiyama Line to Uzumasa Eki. From central or western Kyōto, take Bus 61, 62, or 63 to the Uzumasa-kōryūji-mae stop. *Hachigaoka-chō, Uzumasa, Ukyō-ku. ¥600. Mar.–Nov., daily 9–5; Dec.–Feb., daily 9–4:30.*

★ **38 MYŌSHIN-JI.** Japan's oldest bell—cast in 698—hangs in the belfry near the South Gate of this 14th-century temple. When Emperor Hanazono died, his villa was converted into a temple;

the work required so many laborers that a complex of buildings was built to house them. In all, there are some 40 structures here, though only four are open to the public. Beware of the dragon on the ceiling of Myōshin-ji's Hattō (Lecture Hall). Known as the "Dragon Glaring in Eight Directions," it looks at you wherever you stand.

Within the complex, the temple **Taizō-in** has a famous painting by Sanraku Kanō called *Four Sages of Mt. Shang*, recalling the four wise men who lived in isolation on a mountain to avoid the reign of destruction. The garden of Taizō-in is gentle and quiet—a good place to rest. The temple structure, originally built in 1404, suffered like the rest of the Myōshin-ji complex in the Ōnin Civil War (1467–77) and had to be rebuilt.

Buses 61, 62, and 63 all stop at the Myōshin-ji-mae stop. ¥400 for Myōshin-ji; additional ¥400 for Taizō-in. Daily 9:10–11:50 and 1–4.

★ ㊲ **NINNA-JI.** The original temple here was once the palace of Emperor Omuro, who started the building's construction in 896. Nothing of that structure remains; the complex of buildings that stands today was rebuilt in the 17th century. There's an attractive five-story pagoda (1637), and the Hon-dō (Main Hall), which was moved from the Imperial Palace, is also worth noting as a National Treasure. The temple's focus of worship is the Amida Buddha. Take either Bus 26 or 59 to the Omuro-ninna-ji stop. ¥500. Daily 9–4:30.

★ ㊱ **RYŌAN-JI.** The garden at Ryōan-ji, rather than the temple, attracts people from all over the world. Knowing that the temple belongs to the Rinzai sect of Zen Buddhism may help you appreciate the austere aesthetics of the garden. It's a karesansui, a dry garden: just 15 rocks arranged in three groupings of seven, five, and three in gravel. From the temple's veranda, the proper viewing place, only 14 rocks can be seen at one time. Move slightly and another rock appears and one of the original 14 disappears. In the Buddhist world the number 15 denotes completeness. You must have a total view of the garden to make it a whole and meaningful experience—and yet, in the conditions of this world, that is not possible.

If possible, visit Ryōan-ji in the early morning before the crowds arrive and disturb the garden's contemplative quality. If you need a moment or two to yourself, head to the small restaurant on the temple grounds near an ancient pond, where you can find solace with an expensive beer if need be. From a southbound 12 or 59 bus, the temple will be on your right. *13 Goryoshita-machi, Ryōan-ji, Ukyō-ku. ¥500. Mar.–Nov., daily 8–5; Dec.–Feb., daily 8:30–4:30.*

(39) UZUMASA EIGA MURA (Uzumasa Movie Village). This is Japan's answer to Hollywood, and had Kyōto been severely damaged in World War II, this would have been the last place to glimpse old Japan, albeit as a reproduction. Traditional country villages, ancient temples, and old-fashioned houses make up the stage sets, and if you're lucky, you may catch a couple of actors dressed as samurai snarling at each other, ready to draw their swords. You can visit the stage sets where popular traditional Japanese television series are filmed, or take in the *Red Shadow* action show, based on a popular TV series derived from a comic book. Also part of Eiga Mura is **Padios,** a small amusement park. Eiga Mura is a fine place to bring young children. For adults, whether it's worth the time depends on your interest in Japanese movies and your willingness to give Eiga Mura the two or three hours it takes to visit. The village is on the 61, 62, and 63 bus routes. *10 Higashi-hachigaoka-chō, Uzumasa, tel. 075/881–7716. ¥2,200. Mar.–Nov., daily 9–5; Dec.–Feb., daily 9:30–4.*

ARASHIYAMA AND KATSURA RIKYŪ

The pleasure of Arashiyama, the westernmost part of Kyōto, is the same as it has been for centuries. The gentle foothills of the mountains, covered with cherry and maple trees, are splendid, but it is the bamboo forests that really create the atmosphere of untroubled peace. It's no wonder that the aristocracy of feudal Japan came here to escape the famine, riots, and political intrigue that plagued Kyōto with the decline of the Ashikaga Shogunate a millennium ago.

A Good Tour

The easiest ways to get to Arashiyama are by the JR San-in Main Line from Kyōto Eki to Saga Eki, or via the Keifuku Electric Railway to Arashiyama Eki. South of Arashiyama Eki (Saga Eki is just north of Arashiyama Eki), the Oi-gawa flows under the **TOGETSU-KYŌ-BASHI** ㊶, where you can watch *ukai* (cormorant fishing) July and August evenings. The first temple to visit is **TENRYŪ-JI** ㊷—walk north from Arashiyama Eki or west from JR Saga Eki. One of the best ways to enjoy some contemplative peace is to walk the estate grounds of Denjiro Ōkōchi, a silent-movie actor of samurai films. To reach Ōkōchi's villa, either walk through the temple garden or leave Tenryū-ji and walk north on a narrow street through a **BAMBOO FOREST** ㊸, one of the best you'll see around Kyōto. The **ŌKŌCHI SANSŌ** ㊹ will soon be in front of you. To reach the final two sights on the tour, both south of Arashiyama, you'll need to take the Hankyū Arashiyama Line; the station is south of the Togetsu-kyō-bashi. Head first to Matsuno Eki and the nearby Moss Temple, **KOINZAN SAIHŌ-JI** ㊺, popularly known as Kokedera. Note that you'll need to arrange special permission ahead of time to visit the temple and garden here. The final sight is the imperial villa, **KATSURA RIKYŪ** ㊻, which reaches the heights of cultivated Shoin architecture and garden design. Continue on the Hankyū Arashiyama Line to Katsura Eki. You'll need to make reservations in advance for one of the scheduled guided tours of Katsura. To return to central Kyōto, take the Hankyū Kyōto Line from Katsura Eki to one of the central Kyōto Hankyū stations: Hankyū-Ōmiya, Karasuma, or Kawara-machi.

TIMING

You can see most of Arashiyama in a relaxed morning or afternoon, with the jaunt south to Saihō-ji and Katsura—where you should plan to spend at least an hour at each location—at the beginning or end of the tour.

What to See

43 **BAMBOO FOREST.** Dense bamboo forests provide a feeling of composure and tranquillity quite different from the wooded tracts of the Western world. Nowadays they are few and far between. This one, on the way to Ōkōchi Sansō from Tenryū-ji, is a delight.

★ **46** **KATSURA RIKYŪ** (Katsura Detached Villa). Built in the 17th century for Prince Toshihito, brother of Emperor Go-yōzei, Katsura is beautifully set in southwestern Kyōto on the banks of the Katsura-gawa, with peaceful views of Arashiyama and the Kameyama Hills. Perhaps more than anywhere else in the area, the setting is the most perfect example of Japanese integration of nature and architecture.

Here you'll find Japan's oldest surviving stroll garden. As is typical of the period, the garden makes use of a wide variety of styles, with elements of pond and island, karesansui (dry gardens), and tea gardens, among others. The garden is a study in the placement of stones and the progressive unfolding of the views that the Japanese have so artfully mastered in garden design. Look out from the three shōin (a style of house that incorporates alcoves and platforms for the display of personal possessions) and the four rustic tea arbors around the central pond, which have been strategically placed for optimal vistas. Bridges constructed from earth, stone, and wood connect five islets in the pond.

An extensive network of varied pathways takes you through a vast repertoire of Katsura's miniaturizations of landscapes: an encyclopedia of famous Japanese natural sites and literary references, such as the 11th-century *Tale of Genji*. These associations might be beyond the average foreigner's Japanese education, but what certainly isn't is the experience of the garden that the designer intended for all visitors. Not satisfied to create simply beautiful pictures, Kobori Enshū focused on the rhythm within the garden: spaces open then close, are bright then dark; views are visible and then concealed.

The villa is fairly remote from other historical sites—allow several hours for a visit. Katsura requires special permission for a visit. Applications must be made, preferably a day in advance, in person to the **Imperial Household Agency** (Kyōto Gyoen-nai, Kamigyō-ku, tel. 075/211–1215), open weekdays 8:45–4. You will need your passport to pick up a permit, and you must be at least 20 years of age. The time of your tour will be stated, and you must not be late. The tour is in Japanese only, although a videotape introducing various aspects of the garden in English is shown in the waiting room before each tour begins.

To reach the villa, take the Hankyū Railway Line from one of the Hankyū Kyōto Line stations to Katsura Eki; then walk 15 minutes to the villa from the station's east exit or take a taxi for about ¥600. *Katsura Shimizu-chō, Ukyō-ku, tel. 075/211–1215 (inquiries only). Free. Tours weekdays and 1st and 3rd Sat. of month at 10, 11, 2, and 3; every Sat. in Apr.–May and Oct.–Nov.*

★ ㊺ **KOINZAN SAIHŌ-JI** (Moss Temple). Entrance into the temple precincts transports you into an extraordinary sea of green: 120 varieties of moss create waves of greens and blues that eddy and swirl gently around Koinzan Saihō-ji's garden and give the temple its popular name, Kokedera—the Moss Temple. Surrounded by the multihued moss, many feel the same sense of inner peace that comes from being near water.

The site was originally the villa of Prince Shōtoku (572–621). During the Tempyō era (729–749) the emperor Shōmu charged the priest Gyogi Bosatsu to create 49 temples in the central province, one of which was this temple. The original garden represented Jōdo, the Pure Land, or western paradise of Buddhism. The temple and garden, destroyed many times by fire, lay in disrepair until 1338, when the chief priest of nearby Matsuno-jinja had a revelation here. He convinced Musō Soseki, a distinguished Zen priest of Rinzenji, the head temple of the Rinzai sect of Zen Buddhism, to preside over the temple and convert it from the Jōdo to Zen sect. Soseki, an avid gardener, designed the temple garden on two levels surrounding a pond in the shape of the Chinese character for heart. Present-day visitors are grateful for his efforts. The garden is entirely covered with moss and provides a unique setting for a contemplative walk. May and June, when colors are brightest due to heavy rains, are the best times to see the garden.

Another interesting aspect to your temple visit is the obligatory sha-kyō, writing of sutras. Before viewing the garden, you enter the temple and take a seat at a small, lacquered writing table where you'll be provided with a brush, ink, and a thin sheet of paper with Chinese characters in light gray. After rubbing your ink stick on the ink stone, dip the tip of your brush in the ink and trace over the characters. A priest explains in Japanese the temple history and the sutra you are writing. If time is limited you don't have to write the entire sutra; when the priest has ended his explanation, simply place what you have written on a table before the altar and proceed to the garden.

To gain admission send a stamped, self-addressed postcard to: Saihō-ji Temple, 56 Matsuno Jinjatani-chō, Nishikyō-ku, Kyōto 615-8286. Include the date and time you would like to visit. You can write in English, and the response will also be in English. The postcard must reach the temple at least five days prior to your visit. It's also possible to arrange a visit through the Tourist Information Center. To reach the temple, take the Hankyū Line from Arashiyama to Matsuno Eki. ¥3,000 (have exact change).

ŌKŌCHI SANSŌ. Walk the estate grounds of Ōkōchi's Mountain Villa to breathe in some contemplative peace—Denjiro Ōkōchi, a renowned silent-movie actor of samurai films, chose this location for his home because of the superb views of Arashiyama and Kyōto. Admission to the villa includes tea and cake to enjoy while you absorb nature's pleasures. *8 Tabuchiyama-chō, Ogurayama, Saga, Ukyō-ku, tel. 075/872–2233. ¥900. Daily 9–5.*

★ ㊷ **TENRYŪ-JI.** For good reason is this known as the Temple of the Heavenly Dragon: Emperor Go-Daigo, who had successfully brought an end to the Kamakura Shogunate, was unable to hold on to his power and was forced from his throne by Takauji Ashikaga. After Go-Daigo died, Takauji had twinges of conscience. That's when Priest Musō Sōseki had a dream in which a golden dragon rose from the nearby Oi-gawa. He told the shōgun about his dream and interpreted it to mean the spirit of Go-Daigo was not at peace. Worried that this was an ill omen, Takauji built Tenryū-ji in 1339 on the same spot where Go-Daigo had his favorite villa. Apparently that appeased the spirit of the late emperor. In the Hattō (Lecture Hall), where today's monks meditate, a huge "cloud dragon" is painted on the ceiling. The temple was often ravaged by fire, and the current buildings are as recent as 1900; the painting of the dragon was rendered by 20th-century artist Shōnen Suzuki.

The **Sōgenchi garden** of Tenryū-ji, however, dates from the 14th century and is one of the most notable in Kyōto. Musō Soseki, an influential Zen monk and skillful garden designer, created the garden to resemble Mt. Hōrai in China. It is famed for the arrangement of vertical stones in its large pond and for its role as one of the first gardens to use "borrowed scenery," incorporating the mountains in the distance into the design of the garden.

If you visit Tenryū-ji at lunchtime, consider purchasing a ticket for Zen cuisine served at **Shigetsu,** within the temple precinct. The ¥3,500 price includes lunch in the large dining area overlooking a garden, as well as admission to the garden itself. Here you can experience the Zen monk's philosophy of "eating to live" rather than "living to eat." While you won't be partaking of the monk's daily helping of gruel, a salted plum, and pickled radishes, you will get to try Zen cuisine prepared for festival days. The meal includes sesame tofu served over top-quality soy sauce, a variety of fresh boiled vegetables, miso soup, and rice. The *tenzo*, a monk specially trained to prepare Zen cuisine, creates a multicourse meal that achieves the harmony of the six basic flavors—bitter, sour, sweet, salty, light, and hot—required to enable the monks to practice Zen with the least hindrance to their body and mind. It's an experience not to be missed. Though advance reservations are not required for the ¥3,500 course, there are more elaborate courses for ¥5,500 and ¥7,500 that do require reservations (tel. 075/882–9725); ask someone at your hotel or at the Tourist Information Center to make a reservation for you. Take the JR San-in Main Line from Kyōto Eki to Saga Eki or the Keifuku Electric Railway to Arashiyama Eki. From Saga Eki walk west; from Arashiyama Eki walk north. *68 Susuki-no-bamba-chō, Saga-Tenryū-ji, Ukyō-ku. Garden ¥500; ¥100 additional to enter temple building. Apr.–Oct., daily 8:30–5:30; Nov.–Mar., daily 8:30–5.*

④① TOGETSU-KYŌ-BASHI. Spanning the Oi-gawa, the bridge is a popular spot from which you can watch ukai during the evening in July and August. Fisherfolk use cormorants to scoop up small sweet fish, which are attracted to the light of the flaming torches hung over the boats. The cormorants would swallow the fish for themselves, of course, but small rings around their necks prevent this. After about five fish, the cormorant has more than his gullet can hold. Then the fisherman pulls the bird back on a string, makes the bird regurgitate his catch, and sends him back for more. The best way to watch this spectacle is to join one of the charter passenger boats. Make a reservation using the number below, call the **Japan Travel Bureau** (tel. 075/361–7241), or use your hotel information desk. Take the JR San-in Main Line from Kyōto Eki to Saga Eki or the Keifuku Electric Railway to Arashiyama Eki. The bridge is south of both stations. *Reservations: Arashiyama Tsusen, 14–4 Nakaoshita-chō, Arashiyama, Nishikyō-ku, tel. 075/861–0223 or 075/861–0302. ¥1,400.*

CENTRAL AND SOUTHERN KYŌTO

Central Kyōto is usually easier to explore after eastern and western Kyōto because the sights here are likely to be convenient to your hotel, and you're likely to see each individually rather than combining them into a single itinerary. Treat sights south of Kyōto Eki the same way, choosing the most interesting for a morning or afternoon venture. The two major sights in central Kyōto are Nijō-jō and the Kyōto Gosho, the castle and the Imperial Palace. The latter requires permission, and you must join a guided tour. The most interesting southern Kyōto sights are Tōfuku-ji and Byōdō-in and the tea-producing Uji-shi.

Numbers in the text correspond to numbers in the margin and on the Central Kyōto map.

A Good Tour

The easiest ways to reach **KYŌTO GOSHO** ㊼, the Imperial Palace, are to take the subway to Imadegawa or to take a bus to the Karasuma-Imadegawa stop. You can join the tour of the palace at the Seisho-mon entrance on Karasuma-dōri. You can easily combine Kyōto Gosho with **NIJŌ-JŌ** ㊽, Kyōto residence of the Tokugawa Shogunate, on the same trip. Take the Karasuma subway line from Imadegawa Eki toward Kyōto Eki to Ōike (two stops) and change to the Tōzai subway line. Board the car heading for Nijō and get off at the next stop, Nijō-jō-mae.

For an excursion into the culture of the tea ceremony, make your way west to the **RAKU BIJUTSUKAN** ㊾, a museum that displays the Raku family's tea bowls. For another change of pace, visit

central kyōto

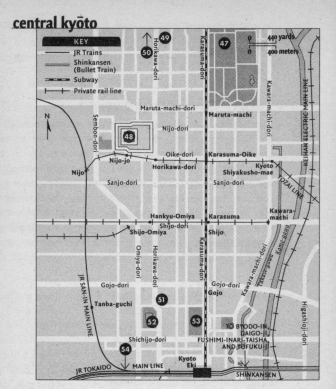

the Nishijin silk-weaving district, north of the Raku Bijutsukan on Horikawa-dōri at the corner of Imadegawa-dōri. At the **NISHIJIN ORIMONO** ⑩, you can watch demonstrations. The Raku Bijutsukan and the Nishijin Orimono are both roughly halfway between the Gosho and Nijō-jō. Buses 9, 12, 50, and 52 run up and down Horikawa-dōri past these two sights.

From the museum, the textile center, or Nijō-jō, take Bus 9 south on Horikawa-dōri. Disembark at the Nishi-Hongan-ji-mae bus stop. Across from the temple, on the fifth floor of the Izutsu Building at the intersection of Horikawa and Shin-Hanaya-chō, is the **FŪZOKU HAKUBUTSUKAN** ⑪, which has clothes that were worn from the pre-Nara era, before 710, to the Meiji period, post-1868. The most famous temples in the area are nearby **NISHI-HONGAN-JI** ⑫ and **HIGASHI-HONGAN-JI** ⑬. Higashi-Hongan-ji is the second-largest wooden structure in Japan. Nishi-Hongan-ji has interesting art objects, but the temple proper requires special permission to enter.

From Nishi-Hongan-ji it's a 10-minute walk southeast to **Kyōto Eki.** Take some time to look around the station building—it's a sight in its own right. If you still have time, visit **TŌ-JI** ⑭, one of Kyōto's oldest temples, southwest of the station. It holds a flea market on the 21st of each month. The best way here is to leave Nishi-Hongan-ji by the west exit and take Bus 207 south on Ōmiya-dōri. Get off at the Tō-ji-Higashimon-mae bus stop, and Tō-ji will be across the street. From Kyōto Eki, Tō-ji is either a 10-minute walk southwest; or you can take the Kintetsu Kyōto Line to Tō-ji Station and walk west for 5 minutes.

Points of interest south of Kyōto Eki require individual trips, returning each time to Kyōto Eki. **Byōdō-in,** a former 10th-century residence turned temple, is in Uji, a famous tea-producing area where you can taste the finest green tea. **Daigo-ji,** in the Yamashina suburb southeast of Kyoto, is a charming 9th-century temple with a five-story pagoda. To reach Daigo-ji, in the southeast suburb of Yamashina, take the Tōzai subway line to Daigo Eki. **Tōfuku-ji,** a Zen temple of the Rinzai sect, ranks as one of the most important Zen temples in Kyōto. It's on the Bus 208 route from Kyōto Eki; or it's a 15-minute walk from Tōfuku-ji Eki on the JR Nara Line or the Keihan Main Line. You may want to combine a visit here with a stop at the **Fushimi-Inari Taisha,** farther south. This shrine is one of Kyōto's oldest and most revered. Fushimi-Inari Taisha is a three-minute walk from the JR Nara Line's Fushimi-Inari Eki.

TIMING

The temples and shrines in southern Kyōto are a distance from one another, so traveling time can eat into your day. But central Kyōto's sights are fairly close to each other and quickly accessible by bus or taxi. A morning would be mostly taken up with the Imperial Palace and Nijō-jō. Remember that the Imperial Palace is closed Saturday afternoon and Sunday, and also all day on the second and fourth Saturday of the month in winter and summer.

What to See

★ **BYŌDŌ-IN.** South of Kyōto in Uji-shi, this temple was originally the villa of a 10th-century member of the influential Fujiwara family. The Amida-dō, also called the Phoenix Hall, was built in the 11th century by the Fujiwaras and is still considered one of Japan's most beautiful religious buildings—something of an architectural folly—where heaven is brought close to earth. Jōchō, one of Japan's most famous 11th-century sculptors, crafted a magnificent statue of a seated Buddha here. **Uji** itself is a famous tea-producing district, and the slope up to the temple is lined with shops where you can sample the finest green tea and pick up a small package to take home. Take the JR Nara line to Uji Eki; from here the temple is a 12-minute walk. *Ujirenge, Uji-shi, tel. 0774/21–2861. ¥500; additional ¥300 for Phoenix Hall. Temple Mar.–Nov., daily 8:30–5:30; Dec.–Feb., daily 9–4:30; Phoenix Hall Mar.–Nov., daily 9–5; Dec.–Feb., daily 9–4.*

★ **DAIGO-JI.** This temple was founded in 874, and over the succeeding centuries other buildings were added and its gardens expanded. Its five-story pagoda, which dates from 951, is reputed to be the oldest existing structure in Kyōto. By the late 16th century the temple had begun to decline in importance and showed signs of neglect. Then Hideyoshi Toyotomi paid a visit one April, when the temple's famous cherry trees were in blossom. Hideyoshi ordered the temple restored. The smaller **Sambo-in** houses paintings by the Kanō school. To reach Daigo-ji, in the southeast suburb of Yamashina, take the Tōzai subway line to Daigo Eki. 22 Higashi Ōji-chō, Fushimi-ku. ¥500. Mar.–Oct., daily 9–5; Nov.–Feb., daily 9–4.

★ **FUSHIMI-INARI TAISHA.** One of Kyōto's oldest and most revered shrines, the Fushimi-Inari honors the goddesses of agriculture (rice and rice wine) and prosperity. It also serves as the headquarters for all the 40,000 shrines representing Inari. The shrine is noted for its bronze foxes and for some 10,000 small torii, donated by the thankful, which stretch up the hill behind the structure. If possible, visit near dusk—you'll be among the only people wandering through the tunnels of torii in the quiet woods, a nearly mystical experience as daylight fades. Take the JR Nara Line to Fushimi-Inari Eki, from which it is a three-minute walk to the shrine. From Tōfuku-ji join the JR train at Tōfuku-ji Eki and go one stop south, toward Nara. 68 Fukakusa Yabu-no-uchi-chō, Fushimi-ku. Free. Daily sunrise–sunset.

★ ⑤ **FŪZOKU HAKUBUTSUKAN** (Kyōto Costume Museum). It's well worth a stop here to marvel at the range of fashion, which starts in the pre-Nara era and works its way up through various historical eras to the Meiji period. The museum is one of the best of its kind and, in its own way, gives an account of the history of Japan. Exhibitions, which change twice a year, highlight a specific period in Japanese history. From the Raku Museum, the Nishijin Textile Center, or Nijō-jō, take Bus 9 south on Horikawa-dōri. Disembark at the Nishi-Hongan-ji-mae bus stop. The museum is on the fifth floor of the Izutsu Building, which is at the intersection of Horikawa and Shin-Hanaya-chō, north of the temple on the other side of the street. *Izutsu Bldg., Shimogyō-ku, tel. 075/342-5345. ¥400. Oct. 9–Sept. 2, Mon.–Sat. 9–5 (closed Apr. 1–8, July 1–8, and Dec. 23–Jan. 6).*

★ ⑤ **HIGASHI-HONGAN-JI.** Until the early 17th century Higashi-Hongan-ji and Nishi-Hongan-ji were one temple. Then Ieyasu Tokugawa took advantage of a rift among the Jōdo Shinshu sect of Buddhism and, to diminish its power, split them apart into two different factions. The original faction has the west temple, Nishi-Hongan-ji, and the latter faction the eastern temple, Higashi-Hongan-ji.

The rebuilt (1895) structure of Higashi-Hongan-ji is the second-largest wooden structure in Japan, after Nara's Daibutsu-den. The **Daishi-dō,** a double-roofed structure, is admirable for its curving, swooping lines. Inside are portraits of all the head abbots of the Jōdo Shinshu sect, but, unfortunately, it contains fewer historical objects of interest than does its rival, Nishi-Hongan-ji. From Kyōto Eki walk 500 yards northwest; from the costume museum walk south on Horikawa-dōri. *Shichijō-agaru, Karasuma-dōri, Shimogyō-ku. Free. Mar.–Oct., daily 5:50–5:30; Nov.–Feb., daily 6:20–4:30.*

KYŌTO EKI. Kyōto's train station, opened in 1997, is more than just the city's central point of arrival and departure: its impressive marble-and-glass structure makes it as significant a building as any of Kyōto's ancient treasures. Hiroshi Hara's modern design was at first controversial, but his use of space and lighting—and the sheer enormity of the final product—eventually won over most of its opponents. The station houses a hotel, a theater, a department store, and dozens of shops and restaurants.

47 KYŌTO GOSHO (Imperial Palace). The present palace, a third-generation construction, was completed in 1855, so it has housed only two emperors, one of whom was the young emperor Meiji before he moved his imperial household to Tōkyō. The original, built for Emperor Kammu to the west of the present site, burned down in 1788. A new palace, modeled after the original, then went up on the present site, but it, too, ended in flames. The Gosho itself is a large but simple wooden building that can hardly be described as palatial. On the one-hour tour, you'll only have a chance for a brief glimpse of the Shishin-den—the hall where the inauguration of emperors and other important imperial ceremonies take place—and a visit to the gardens. Though a trip to the Imperial Palace is on most people's agenda and though it fills a fair amount of space in downtown Kyōto, it holds somewhat less interest than do some of the older historic buildings in the city.

Guided tours start at the Seisho-mon entrance. You must arrive at the Imperial Palace before 9.40 AM for the one-hour 10 AM guided tour in English. Present yourself, along with your passport, at the office of the **Kunaichō** (Imperial Household Agency) in the palace grounds. For the 2 PM guided tour in English, arrive by 1:40 PM. The Kunaichō office is closed on weekends, so visit in advance to arrange a Saturday tour. To get to the palace, take the Karasuma Line of the subway in the direction of Kokusaikaikan. Get off at Imadegawa Station, and use the Number 6 Exit. Cross the street and turn right. Enter the palace through the Inui Go-mon on your left. *Kunaichō, Kyōto Gyoen-nai, Kamigyō-ku, tel. 075/211–1215 (information only). Free. Office weekdays 8:45–12 and 1–4; tours weekdays at 10 AM and 2 PM (Sat. tours on 1st and 3rd Sat. of month; every Sat. in Apr.–May and Oct.–Nov.).*

★ **48 NIJŌ-JŌ.** Nijō-jō was the local Kyōto address for the Tokugawa Shogunate. Dominating central Kyōto, it's an intrusion, both politically and artistically. The man who built the castle in 1603, Ieyasu Tokugawa, did so to emphasize that political power had been completely removed from the emperor and that he alone determined the destiny of Japan. As if to emphasize that statement, Tokugawa built and decorated his castle with such ostentation as to make the populace cower in the face of his wealth and power. This kind of display was antithetical to the refined restraint of Kyōto's aristocracy.

Ieyasu Tokugawa had risen to power through skillful political maneuvers and treachery. His military might was unassailable, and that is probably why his Kyōto castle had relatively modest exterior defenses. However, as he well knew, defense against treachery is never certain. The interior of the castle was built with that in mind. Each building had concealed rooms where bodyguards could maintain a watchful eye for potential assassins, and the corridors had built-in "nightingale" floors, so no one could walk in the building without making noise. Rooms were locked only from the inside, thus no one from the outer rooms could gain access to the inner rooms without someone admitting them. The outer rooms were kept for visitors of low rank and were adorned with garish paintings that would impress them. The inner rooms were for the important lords, whom the shōgun would impress with the refined, tasteful paintings of the Kanō school.

The opulence and grandeur of the castle were, in many ways, a snub to the emperor. They relegated the emperor and his palace to insignificance, and the Tokugawa family even appointed a governor to manage the emperor and the imperial family. The Tokugawa shōguns were rarely in Kyōto. Ieyasu stayed in the castle three times, the second shōgun twice, including the time in 1626 when Emperor Gomizuno-o was granted an audience. After that, for the next 224 years, no Tokugawa shōgun visited Kyōto, and the castle started to fall into disrepair and neglect. Only when the Tokugawa Shogunate was under pressure from a failing economy, and international pressure developed to open Japan to trade, did the 14th shōgun, Iemochi Tokugawa (1846–

66), come to Kyōto to confer with the emperor. The emperor told the shōgun to rid Japan of foreigners, but Iemochi did not have the strength. As the shōgun's power continued to wane, the 15th and last shōgun, Keiki Tokugawa (1837–1913), spent most of his time in Nijō-jō. Here he resigned, and the imperial decree was issued that abolished the shogunate after 264 years of rule.

After the Meiji Restoration in 1868, Nijō-jō became the Kyōto prefectural office until 1884; during that time it suffered from acts of vandalism. Since 1939 the castle has belonged to the city of Kyōto, and considerable restoration work has taken place.

You enter the castle through the impressive **Kara-mon** (Chinese Gate). Notice that you must turn right and left at sharp angles to make this entrance—a common attribute of Japanese castles, designed to slow the advance of any attacker. From the Kara-mon, the carriageway leads to the **Ni-no-maru Goten** (Second Inner Palace), whose five buildings are divided into many chambers. The outer buildings were for visits by men of lowly rank, the inner ones for those of higher rank. The most notable room, the **Ōhiroma** (Great Hall), is easy to recognize. In the room, costumed figures reconstruct the occasion when Keiki Tokugawa returned the power of government to the emperor. This spacious hall was where, in the early 17th century, the shōgun would sit on a raised throne to greet important visitors seated below him. The sliding screens of this room have magnificent paintings of forest scenes.

Even more impressive than the palace itself is its garden, created by landscape designer Kobori Enshū shortly before Emperor Gomizuno-o's visit in 1626. Notice the crane-and-tortoise islands flanking the center island (called the Land of Paradise). The symbolic meaning is clear: strength and longevity. The garden was originally designed with no deciduous trees, for the shōgun did not wish to be reminded of the transitory nature of life by autumn's falling leaves.

The other major building on the grounds is the **Hon-maru Palace,** a replacement of the original, which burned down in the 18th century. It's not normally open to the public. To reach the castle, take the bus or subway to Nijō-jō-mae. *Horikawa Nishi-Iru, Nijō-dōri, Nakagyō-ku, tel. 075/841–0096. ¥600. Daily 8:45–5 (last entry at 4).*

NEED A BREAK? After your visit to the palace take a break at the traditional Japanese candy store **Mukashi Natsukashi,** on the corner of Ōmiya-dōri, three blocks west of the intersection of Horikawa-dōri and Oike-dōri. Browse through the quaint candy store, grab a cold drink from a cedar bucket filled with cold water, and try the specialty of the house, *dorobo* (a crispy molasses-covered rice-flour snack). You can rest on the bench outside the shop while sampling your wares. *Oshikoji-dōri, Ōmiya-dōri, Nakagyō-ku. tel. 075/841–4464.*

★ ❺❷ **NISHI-HONGAN-JI.** The marvelous artifacts at this temple were confiscated by Ieyasu Tokugawa from Hideyoshi Toyotomi's Jurakudai Palace, in Kyōto, and from Fushimi-jō, in southern Kyōto. He had the buildings dismantled in an attempt to erase the memory of his predecessor.

Hideyoshi Toyotomi was quite a man. Though most of the initial work in unifying Japan was accomplished by the warrior Nobunaga Oda (he was ambushed a year after defeating the monks on Hiei-zan), it was Hideyoshi who completed the job. Not only did he end civil strife, he also restored the arts. For a brief time (1582–98), Japan entered one of the most colorful periods of its history. How Hideyoshi achieved his feats is not exactly known. He was brought up as a farmer's son, and his nickname was Saru-san (Mr. Monkey) because he was small and ugly. According to one legend—probably started by Hideyoshi himself—he was the son of the emperor's concubine. She had been much admired by a man to whom the emperor owed a favor, so the emperor gave the concubine to him. Unknown to either of the men, she was soon pregnant with Hideyoshi. Whatever his origins (he changed his name frequently), he brought peace to Japan after decades of civil war.

Because much of what was dear to Hideyoshi Toyotomi was destroyed by the Tokugawas, it is only at Nishi-Hongan-ji that you can see the artistic works closely associated with his personal life, including the great **Kara-mon** (Chinese Gate) and the **Daisho-in,** both brought from Fushimi-jō, and the **Nō stage** from Jurakudai Palace.

Nishi-Hongan-ji is on Horikawa-dōri, a couple of blocks north of Shichijō-dōri. Visits to some of the buildings are permitted four times a day by permission from the temple office. Phone for an appointment once you arrive in Kyōto; if you don't speak Japanese, you may want to ask your hotel to place the call for you. Tours of Daisho-in (in Japanese) are given occasionally throughout the year. *Shichijō-agaru, Horikawa-dōri, Shimogyō-ku, tel. 075/371–5181. Free. Mar.–Apr. and Sept.–Oct., daily 5:30–5:30; May–Aug., daily 5:30 AM–6 PM; Nov.–Feb., daily 6–5.*

50 **NISHIJIN ORIMONO** (Textile Center). The Nishijin district still hangs on to the artistic thread of traditional Japanese silk weaving. Nishijin Orimono hosts demonstrations of age-old weaving techniques and presents fashion shows and special exhibitions. On the mezzanine you can buy kimonos and gift items, such as *happi* (workmen's) coats and silk purses. The center is on the 9 and 12 bus routes, north of the Raku Bijutsukan, at the corner of Horikawa-dōri and Imadegawa-dōri. *Horikawa-dōri, Imadegawa-Minami-Iru, Kamigyō-ku, tel. 075/451–9231. Free, kimono show ¥600. Daily 9–5. Closed Aug. 13–15, Dec. 29–Jan. 15.*

49 **RAKU BIJUTSUKAN.** Any serious collector of tea-ceremony artifacts is likely to have a Raku bowl in his or her collection. Here you'll find tea bowls made by members of the Raku family, whose roots can be traced to the 16th century. As a potter's term in the West, *raku* refers to a low-temperature firing technique, but the word originated with this family, who made exquisite tea bowls for use in the shōgun's tea ceremonies. The museum is to the east of Horikawa-dōri, two blocks south of Imadegawa-dōri; take Bus 9 or 12 to Ichi-jō-modōri-bashi. *Aburakōji, Nakadachuri-agaru, Kamigyō-ku, tel. 075/414–0304. ¥700–¥1,000 (depending on exhibition). Tues.–Sun. 10–4:30.*

★ **TŌFUKU-JI.** In all, two dozen subtemples and the main temple compose the complex of this Rinzai-sect Zen temple, established in 1236, which ranks as one of the most important in Kyōto, along with the Myōshin-ji and Daitoku-ji. Autumn is an especially fine time for visiting, when the burnished colors of the maple trees add to the pleasure of the gardens. There are at least three ways to get to Tōfuku-ji, which is southeast of Kyōto Eki: Bus 208 from Kyōto Eki, a JR train on the Nara Line to Tōfuku-ji Eki, or a Keihan Line train to Tōfuku-ji Eki. From the trains, it's a 15-minute walk to the temple. Consider combining a visit here with one to Fushimi-Inari Taisha, farther south. *Honmachi 15-chōme, Higashiyama-ku. ¥400. Daily 9–4.*

54 **TŌ-JI.** Established by imperial edict in 796 and called Kyō-ō-gokoku-ji, Tō-ji was built to guard the city. It was one of the only two temples that Emperor Kammu permitted to be built in the city—he had had enough of the powerful Buddhists during his days in Nara. The temple was later given to Priest Kūkai (Kōbō Daishi), who founded the Shingon sect of Buddhism. Tō-ji became one of Kyōto's most important temples.

Fires and battles during the 16th century destroyed the temple buildings, but many were rebuilt, including the Kon-dō (Main Hall) in 1603. The Kō-dō (Lecture Hall), on the other hand, has managed to survive the ravages of war since it was built in 1491. Inside this hall are 15 original statues of Buddhist gods that were carved in the 8th and 9th centuries. Perhaps Tōji's most eye-catching building is the 180-ft, five-story pagoda, reconstructed in 1695.

An interesting time to visit the temple is on the 21st of each month, when a market, known locally as Kōbō-san, is held. Antique kimonos, fans, and other memorabilia can sometimes be found at bargain prices if you know your way around the savvy dealers. Many elderly people flock to the temple on this day to pray to Kōbō Daishi and to shop. A smaller antiques market is held on the first Sunday of the month. From Kyōto Eki take the Kintetsu Kyōto Line one stop to Tō-ji Eki or walk 10 minutes west from the central exit of JR Kyōto Eki. Bus 207 also runs past Tō-ji: either south from Gion, then west; or west from Karasuma-dōri along Shijō-dōri, then south. Get off at the Tō-ji-Higashimon-mae stop. 1 Kujō-chō, Minami-ku. Main buildings ¥500, grounds free. Mar. 20–Sept. 19, daily 9–5; Sept. 20–Mar. 19, daily 9–4:30.

NORTHERN KYŌTO

Hiei-zan and Ōhara are the focal points in the northern suburbs of Kyoto. Ōhara was for several centuries a sleepy Kyōto backwater surrounded by mountains. Although it is now catching up with the times, it still has a feeling of old Japan, with several temples that deserve visits. Hiei-zan is a fount of Kyōto history. On its flanks Saichō founded Enryaku-ji and with it the vital Tendai sect of Buddhism. It's an essential Kyōto site, and walking on forested slopes among its 70-odd temples is one reason to make the trek to Hiei-zan.

A Good Tour

To get to Ōhara, take private Kyōto Line Bus 17 or 18 from Kyōto Eki and get out at the Ōhara bus stop. The trip takes 90 minutes and costs ¥480. From the bus station, walk northeast for about seven minutes along the signposted road to **Sanzen-in,** a small Tendai-sect temple on delightful grounds with a remarkable carved Amida Buddha. Two hundred yards from Sanzen-in sits the quiet **Jikkō-in,** where you can drink traditional matcha (powdered ceremonial tea). On the other side of Ōhara and the

★ Takano-gawa is **Jakkō-in,** a romantic temple full of pathos and a sanctuary for nuns. To get here, return to the Ōhara bus stop and walk 20 minutes north up the road.

The next stop is **Hiei-zan.** Take Kyōto Line Bus 16, 17, or 18 down the main highway, Route 367, to the Yase Yuenchi bus stop, next to Yase Yuen Eki. You'll see the entrance to the cable car on your left. It departs every 30 minutes, and you can transfer to the ropeway at Hiei for the remaining distance to the top. At the summit is an observatory with panoramic views of the mountains and of Biwa-ko (Lake Biwa). From the observatory, a mountain path leads to **Enryaku-ji,** an important center of Buddhism. Before day's end, return from Hiei-zan by taking the Eizan Railway from Yase Yuen Eki to Shūgaku-in Eki and making a 15-minute walk to the **Shūgaku-in Rikyū,** which consists of a complex of three palaces. The return to central Kyōto takes an hour on Bus 5 to Kyōto Eki or 20 minutes by Keifuku Eizan train to Demachi-Yanagi Eki, just north of Imadegawa-dōri.

One final sight, closer to central Kyōto, is **Kamigamo Jinja,** built by the legendary warrior Kamo. It's near the end of the Bus 9 route north from Kyōto Eki by the Kamigamo-Misonobashi stop.

TIMING

It's best to make this a day trip to allow for unhurried exploration of Ōhara and on Hiei-zan. If you're short on time, you could cover the sights in about four hours.

What to See

HIEI-ZAN AND ENRYAKU-JI. From the observatory at the top of Hiei-zan, a serpentine mountain path leads to Enryaku-ji, which remains a vital center of Buddhism. At one time it consisted of 3,000 buildings and had its own standing army. That was its downfall. Enryaku-ji really began in 788. Emperor Kammu, the founding father of Kyōto, requested Priest Saichō (767–822) to establish a temple on Hiei-zan to protect the area (including Nagaoka, then the capital) from the evil spirits. Demons and evil spirits were thought to come from the northeast, and Hiei-zan was a natural barrier between the fledgling city and the northeastern Kin-mon (Devil's Gate), where devils were said to pass. The temple's monks were to serve as lookouts and, through their faith, keep evil at bay.

The temple grew, and because police were not allowed on its mountaintop sanctuary, criminals flocked here, ostensibly to seek salvation. By the 11th century the temple had formed its own army to secure order on its estate. In time, this army grew and became stronger than that of most other feudal lords, and the power of Enryaku-ji came to threaten Kyōto. No imperial army could manage a war without the support of Enryaku-ji, and when there was no war, Enryaku-ji's armies would burn and slaughter monks of rival Buddhist sects. Not until the 16th century was there a force strong enough to sustain an assault on the temple. With accusations that the monks had concubines and never read the sutras, Nobunaga Oda (1534–82), the general who unified Japan by ending more than a century of civil strife, attacked the monastery in 1571 to rid it of its evil. In the battle, monks were killed, and most of the buildings were destroyed. Structures standing today were built in the 17th century.

Enryaku-ji has three main precincts: the Eastern Precinct, where the main building in the complex, the **Kompon Chū-dō**, stands; the Western Precinct, with the oldest building, the **Shaka-dō**; and the Yokawa district, a few miles north. The Kompon Chū-dō dates from 1642, and its dark, cavernous interior quickly conveys the sense of mysticism for which the esoteric Tendai sect is known. Giant pillars and a coffered ceiling shelter the central altar, which is surrounded by religious images and sacred objects. The ornate lanterns that hang before the altar are said to have been lighted by Saichō himself centuries ago.

The Western precinct is where Saichō founded his temple and where he is buried. An incense burner wafts smoke before his tomb, which lies in a small hollow. The peaceful atmosphere of the cedar trees surrounding the main structures—Jōdo-in, Ninai-dō, and Shaka-dō—suggests an imitation of the essence of the life of a Tendai Buddhist monk, who devotes his life to the esoteric. Enryaku-ji is still an important training ground for Buddhism, on a par with the temples at Kōya-san. The value of coming here is in experiencing Enryaku-ji's overall aura of spiritual profundity rather than its particular buildings. Though the temple complex is only a 20th of its original size, the magnitude of the place and the commitment to esoterica pursued here are awesome.

Take Kyōto Line Bus 16, 17, or 18 up the main highway, Route 367, to the Yase Yuenchi bus stop, next to Yase Yuen Eki. You'll see the entrance to the cable car on your left. It departs every 30 minutes, and you can transfer to the ropeway at Hiei for the remaining ride to the summit, where an observatory affords panoramic views of the mountains and of Biwa-ko. *Enryaku-ji: 4220 Sakamoto-hon-machi, Ōtsu-shi. Enryaku-ji ¥800; Hiei-zan cable car ¥530, ropeway ¥310. Enryaku-ji Mar.–Nov., daily 8:30–4:30; Dec.–Feb., daily 9–4. Hiei-zan ropeway Apr.–Sept., daily 9–6; Oct.–Mar., daily 9–5 (mid-July–late Aug., observatory open until 9).*

★ **JAKKŌ-IN.** In April 1185 the Taira clan met its end in a naval battle against the Minamoto clan. For two years Yoshitsune Minamoto had been gaining the upper hand in the battles. In this one, the Minamotos slaughtered the Tairas, turning the Seto Nai-kai (Inland Sea) red with Taira blood. Recognizing that all was lost, the Taira women drowned themselves, taking with them the young infant Emperor Antoku. His mother, Kenreimonin, too, leaped into the sea, but Minamoto soldiers snagged her hair with a grappling hook and hauled her back on board their ship. She was the sole surviving member of the Taira clan and, at 29, she was a beautiful woman.

Taken back to Kyōto, Kenreimonin shaved her head and became a nun. First, she had a small hut at Chōraku-ji in eastern Kyōto, and when that collapsed in an earthquake, she was accepted at Jakkō-in. She lived in solitude in a 10-ft-square cell made of brushwood and thatch for 27 years, until death erased her memories and with her the Taira. Her mausoleum is in the temple grounds.

When Kenreimonin came to Jakkō-in, it was far removed from Kyōto. Now Kyōto's sprawl reaches this far and beyond, but the temple, hidden in trees, is still a place of solitude and a sanctuary for nuns. From Kyōto Eki take Kyōto Line Bus 17 or 18 for a 90-minute ride and get out at the Ōhara bus stop; the fare is ¥480. Walk 20 minutes or so along the road leading to the northwest. ¥500. Mar.–Jan., daily 9–5; Dec.–Feb., daily 9–4:30.

★ **JIKKŌ-IN.** At this small, little-frequented temple you can sit, relax, and have a taste of the powdered matcha of the tea ceremony. To enter, ring the gong on the outside of the gate and then wander through the carefully cultivated garden. Take Kyōto Line Bus 17 or 18 for 90 minutes from Kyōto Eki; the fare is ¥580. From the Ōhara bus stop, walk northeast for about seven minutes along the signposted road. Jikkō-in is 200 yards from Sanzen-in. ¥500. Daily 9–5.

KAMIGAMO JINJA. The warrior Kamo built Kamigamo and its sister shrine, Shimogamo Jinja (farther south on the Kamogawa), in the 8th century. Such is Kamo's fame that even the river that flows by the shrine and through the center of Kyōto bears his name. Kamigamo has always been associated with Wakeikazuchi, a god of thunder, rain, and fertility. Now the shrine is famous for its Aoi (Hollyhock) Festival, which started in the 6th century when people thought that the Kamigamo deities were angry at being neglected. Held every May 15, the festival consists of 500 people wearing Heian-period costumes riding on horseback or in ox-drawn carriages from the Imperial Palace to Shimogamo and then to Kamigamo. To get to the shrine, take

Bus 9 north from Kyōto Eki or from a stop on Horikawa-dōri. Or take the subway north to Kitayama Eki, from which the shrine is 20 minutes on foot northwest. *Motoyama, Kamigamo, Kita-ku. Free. Daily 9–4:30.*

MIHO BIJUTSUKAN (Miho Museum). Built in and around a mountaintop and thoughtfully landscaped—its wooded setting in the hills of Shigariki north of Kyōto is part of the experience of a visit here—the I. M. Pei–designed Miho Museum houses the remarkable Shumei family collection of traditional Japanese art and Asian and Western antiquities. An Egyptian falcon-headed deity, a Roman fresco, a Chinese tea bowl, and a Japanese Bosatsu (Buddha) are among the superb pieces here. A restaurant on-site sells bentō with organic ingredients, and a tearoom serves Japanese and Western beverages and desserts. From Kyōto Eki take the JR Tōkaidō Line (¥230 to Ishiyama Eki, 15 minutes); from here the bus to the museum will take 50 minutes. There are only two buses a day, at 9:10 AM and 11:55 AM during the week; bus service is extended on weekends and public holidays. *300 Momodani, Shigariki, tel. 0748/82–3411. ¥1,000. Mid-Mar.–mid-June and Sept.–mid-Dec., Tues.–Sun. 10–5 (last entry at 4).*

SANZEN-IN. This small temple of the Tendai sect was founded by a renowned priest, Dengyo-Daishi (767–822). The Hon-dō (Main Hall) was built by Priest Eshin (942–1017), who probably carved the temple's Amida Buddha—though some say it was carved 100 years after Eshin's death. Flanked by two disciples, Daiseishi and Kannon, the statue is a remarkable piece of work, because rather than representing the bountiful Amida, it displays much more the omnipotence of Amida. Although Eshin was not a master sculptor, this statue possibly reflects his belief that, contrary to the prevailing belief of the Heian aristocracy that salvation could be achieved through one's own actions, salvation could be achieved only through Amida's limitless mercy. The statue is in the Main Hall. Unusual for a Buddhist temple, Sanzen-in faces east, not south. Note its ceiling, on which a painting depicts the descent of Amida, accompanied by 25 bodhisattvas, to welcome the believer.

The grounds are also delightful. Full of maple trees, the gardens are serene in any season. During autumn the colors are magnificent, and the approach to the temple up a gentle slope enhances the anticipation for the burned gold trees guarding the old, weathered temple. Snow cover in winter is also magical. Take Kyōto Line Bus 17 or 18 north for 90 minutes from Kyōto Eki; the fare is ¥580. From the Ōhara bus station walk northeast for about seven minutes along the signposted road. *Raigōin-chō, Ōhara, Sakyō-ku. ¥600. Mar.–Nov., daily 8:30–4:30; Dec.–Feb., daily 8:30–4.*

SHŪGAKU-IN RIKYŪ (Shūgaku-in Imperial Villa). Three palaces make up this villa complex with pleasant grounds. The Upper and Lower villas were built in the 17th century by the Tokugawa family to entertain the emperor. The Upper Villa provides nice views. The Middle Villa was added later as a palace home for Princess Ake, daughter of Emperor Gosai. When she decided that a nun's life was her calling, the villa was transformed into a temple.

Special permission is required to visit the villa from the Imperial Household Agency, preferably a day in advance. From Hiei-zan take the Eizan Railway from Yase Yuen Eki to Shūgaku-in Eki. The villa is a 15-minute walk from here. From central Kyōto the trip takes an hour on Bus 5 from Kyōto Eki. Or take the 20-minute ride north on a Keifuku Eizan Line train from the Demachi-Yanagi terminus, which is just northeast of the intersection of Imadegawa-dōri and the Kamo-gawa. *Yabusoe Shūgaku-in, Sakyō-ku. Free. Tours (in Japanese only) weekdays at 9, 10, 11, 1:30, and 3 (Sat. tours on 1st and 3rd Sat. of month; every Sat. Apr.–May and Oct.–Nov.).*

In This Chapter

Updated by Lauren Sheridan

eating out

"PARIS EAST" IS A DIFFICULT EPITHET FOR KYŌTO TO LIVE UP TO, but in many ways the elegant sister cities do seem to be of the same flesh and blood—not least in that both serve up their nation's haute cuisine. The presence of the imperial court was the original inspiration for Kyōto's exclusive *yusoku ryōri*. Once presented on lacquered pedestals to the emperor himself, it is now offered at but one restaurant in the city, Mankamero.

The experience not to miss in Kyōto is *kaiseki ryōri*, the elegant full-course meal that was originally intended to be served with the tea ceremony. All the senses are engaged in this culinary event: the scent and flavor of the freshest ingredients at the peak of season; the visual delight of a continuous procession of porcelain dishes and lacquered bowls, each a different shape and size, gracefully adorned with an appropriately shaped morsel of fish or vegetable; the textures of foods unknown and exotic, presented in sequence to prevent boredom; the sound of water in a stone basin outside in the garden. Even the atmosphere of the room enhances the experience: a hanging scroll displayed in the alcove and a carefully crafted flower arrangement evoke the season and accent the restrained appointments of the tatami room. Kaiseki ryōri is often costly yet always unforgettable.

For an initiation or a reasonably priced sample, the *kaiseki bentō* (box lunch) served by many *ryōtei* (high-class Japanese restaurants) is a good place to start. Box lunches are so popular in Kyōto that restaurants compete to make their bentō unique, exquisite, and delicious.

Because it is a two-day journey from the sea, Kyōto is historically more famous for ingenious ways of serving preserved fish—dried, salted, or pickled—than for its raw-fish dishes, though with modern transport have come good sushi shops. Compared with the style of cooking elsewhere in Japan, Kyōto-ryōri (Kyōto cuisine) is lighter and more delicate, stressing the natural flavor of ingredients over enhancement with heavy sauces and broths. Tsukemono (pickled vegetables) and wagashi (traditional sweets) are two other local specialties; they make excellent souvenirs. Food shops are often kept just as they were a century ago—well worth the trip if only to browse.

Kyōto is also the home of shōjin ryōri, the Zen vegetarian-style cooking, best sampled on the grounds of one of the city's Zen temples, such as Tenryū-ji in Arashiyama. Local delicacies like fu (glutinous wheat cakes) and yuba (soy-milk skimmings) have found their way into the mainstream of Kyōto-ryōri but were originally devised to provide protein in the traditional Buddhist diet.

Most of Kyōto's restaurants accept credit cards; however, some of the finest traditional restaurants do not, so it's wise to check ahead, especially since traditional kaiseki ryōri can be quite expensive. People generally dine early in Kyōto, between 7 PM and 8 PM, so most restaurants apart from hotel restaurants and bars close relatively early. In some cases this means 7, though most are open until 9. The average Japanese businessman wears a suit and tie to dinner—anywhere. Young people tend to dress more informally. If you think that you'll feel uncomfortable without a jacket, take one along. Many Kyōto restaurants do have someone who speaks English if it turns out that you need assistance making reservations.

Kyōto has its share of the sort of budget quasi-Western–style chain restaurants found all over Japan, serving sandwiches and salads, gratins, curried rice, and spaghetti. These are easy to locate along Kawara-machi-dōri downtown, and they usually come complete with plastic models in the window to which you can point if spoken language fails you.

CATEGORY	COST*
$$$$	over ¥12,000
$$$	¥6,500–¥12,000
$$	¥2,500 ¥6,500
$	under ¥2,500

*per person for a main course at dinner

EASTERN KYŌTO

Japanese

$$$$ **KIKUSUI.** Near Nanzen-ji temple, Kikusui serves up traditional kaiseki ryōri and a view of an elegant Japanese stroll garden. The colors of Nanzen-ji-michi are particularly beautiful in the spring, when a large, umbrella-like cherry tree spreads its pink and white blossoms overhead like a canopy. Autumn, when maples explode in a firework display of reds and oranges, is also lovely. You can sample the subtle flavors and beautiful colors of Kyōto's traditional cuisine by ordering the kyō-no-aji (mini kaiseki) at lunchtime for a reasonable ¥5,000. 31 Fukui-cho, Nazenji, Sakyō-ku, tel. 075/771-4101. Reservations essential. AE, DC, V.

$$$–$$$$ **ASHIYA STEAK HOUSE.** A short walk from the Gion district, famous for its teahouses and geisha, Ashiya Steak House is the best place in Kyōto to enjoy "a good steak . . . a real martini . . . and the essence of traditional Japan," in the words of owner Bob Strickland and his wife, Tokiko. While you're seated at a kotatsu (recessed hearth), your teppanyaki dinner of the finest Ōmi beefsteak, grilled and sliced in style, will be prepared as you watch. Cocktails, domestic and imported wines, and beer are available, as well as the best sake. You can take cocktails in the art gallery upstairs, which has a display of traditional and contemporary arts and crafts. 172–13 4-chōme, Kiyomizu,

kyōto dining

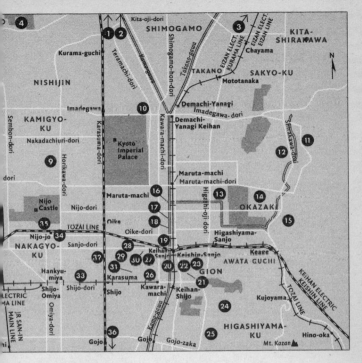

Higashiyama-ku, tel. 075/541–7961. *Reservations essential. AE, DC, V. Closed Mon.*

$$$–$$$$ MATSUNO. Eel may not sound very appetizing at first, but the appeal of *unagi* is slightly more obvious. Once most visitors taste the succulent broiled fish served in its own special sweet sauce, they don't feel so squeamish. Two doors down from the Kabuki theater Minami-za, Matsuno serves unagi to an after-theater crowd in simple but elegant surroundings. Its prices match its century-old reputation; try the *unagi-domburi* (grilled eel on rice) for a simple (and cheaper) version of this delicacy. *Minamiza-higashi 4-ken-me, Shijō-dōri, Higashiyama-ku, tel. 075/561–2786. MC, V. Closed Thurs.*

$$–$$$$ NONTARO. If you're looking for a great sushi experience in the heart of the geisha district, try popular Nontaro, which has been serving sushi to visitors to Gion for more than 40 years. You can order sushi à la carte or choose one of the *omakase* (chef's choice) selections. If you're in the mood for something different, try the *kokesushi*—a giant sushi roll. *Hanamikō-ji Shijō-agaru, Higashiyama-ku, tel. 075/561–3189. Reservations essential. AE, DC, MC, V. Closed Sun.*

$$–$$$$ ROKUSEI NISHIMISE. Few restaurants in Kyōto have matched Rokusei Nishimise's magical combination of traditional cuisine and contemporary setting. Polished marble floors and manicured interior-garden niches complement the popular ¥3,000 *te-oke bentō* lunch, a collage of flavors and colors presented on a serving tray that's a handmade cypress-wood bucket. With a history as a caterer of formal kaiseki cuisine that began in 1899, Rokusei also serves a different, exquisite, full-course meal each month for ¥10,000—expensive, you may say, but in the world of Kyōto's haute cuisine, this is reasonable. The restaurant, a three-minute walk west of the turn-of-the-20th-century gardens of the Heian Jingū, overlooks a tree-lined canal and is famous for its colorful azaleas in May. *71 Nishitennō-chō, Okazaki, Sakyō-ku, tel. 075/751–6171. AE, DC, V. Closed Mon.*

$$–$$$ **YAGEMBORI.** North of Shijō-dōri in the heart of Kyōto's still-
★ thriving geisha district, this restaurant is in a teahouse just a few
steps down a cobbled path from the romantic Shira-kawa, a small
tributary of the Kamo-gawa, in Gion. The *omakase* full-course
meal is an elegant sampler of Kyōto's finest kaiseki cuisine, with
local delicacies presented on handmade ceramics. The *shabu-
shabu* (thinly sliced beef, dipped briefly into hot stock) and *suppon*
(turtle dishes) are excellent. Don't miss the *hoba miso*—bean
paste with *kinoko* mushrooms and green onions, which are wrapped
in a giant oak leaf and grilled at your table—on the à la carte menu.
*Sueyoshi-chō, Kiridoshi-kado, Gion, Higashiyama-ku, tel. 075/551–
3331. AE, DC, V.*

$$ **OMEN.** Just south of Ginkaku-ji, this is one of the best places to
★ stop for an inexpensive home-style lunch before proceeding down
the old canal—the walkway beneath the cherry trees known as
the Path of Philosophy—on the way to Nanzen-ji. Omen is not
only the name of the shop but also the name of the house specialty:
thick white noodles brought to your table in a basket with a bowl
of hot broth and a platter of seven vegetables. The noodles—along
with vegetables such as spinach, cabbage, green onions,
mushrooms, burdock root, eggplant, radishes, and others,
depending on the season—are added to the broth a little at a time.
Sprinkle the top with roasted sesame seeds, and you have a dish
so popular that you can expect a few minutes' wait before you're
seated. Like the food, the restaurant is country style, with a choice
of counter stools, tables and chairs, or tatami mats. The waiters
dress in *happi* coats and headbands; the atmosphere is lively and
comfortable. Reservations are only accepted on weekdays. *74 Ishi-
bashi-chō, Jōdo-ji, Sakyō-ku, tel. 075/771–8994. No credit cards. Closed
Thurs.*

$–$$ **GRILL KODAKARA.** Although you may recognize the names on
the menu, you probably won't recognize the dishes themselves.
Locals consider the food served at this clean, quiet restaurant on
Okazaki-michi near Heian Jingū to be Western, but it has a

Japanese flair that comes from its subtle yet rich demi-glace sauce. The sauce, which is stewed for five days to bring out its full flavor, is used in the beef stew, hashed-beef rice, and rice omelet. For a small fee, you can take home a Grill Kodakara Print Club sticker with your photo as a souvenir. 46 Kitagosho-chō, Okazaki, Sakyō-ku, tel. 075/771–5893. MC, V. Closed Wed.

$ **RAKUSHŌ.** Flowering plum trees, azaleas, irises, camellias, and
★ maple trees take turns coloring the four seasons while countless visitors slip in and out, sipping bowls of frothy matcha or freshly brewed coffee and taking in the scenery. Along the path between Maruyama Kōen and Kiyomizu-dera, this tea shop in a former villa is a pleasant place to stop for morning coffee or afternoon tea. You can also order warabi mochi, a dessert that resembles Jell-O in a sweet, sticky sauce. A table beside the sliding glass doors looks out on an elaborately landscaped garden; in the pond in the garden, the owner's colorful prize-winning koi (carp) lurk just beneath the surface. The tea shop is minutes on foot from Sannen-zaka, one of Kyōto's historic preservation districts—a cobblestone path lined with shops on the way to Kiyomizu-dera. Rakushō closes at 6 PM. Kōdai-ji Kitamon-mae-dōri, Washio-chō, Higashiyama-ku, tel. 075/561–6892. Reservations not accepted. No credit cards. Closed 4 times a month (call ahead).

WESTERN KYŌTO

Japanese

$$$$ **KITCHO.** What Maxim's is to Paris, Kitcho is to Kyōto—classic cuisine, an unparalleled traditional atmosphere, exclusive elegance. Lunch here starts at ¥45,000, dinner at ¥50,000, making this perhaps the world's most expensive restaurant. Although the original restaurant is in Ōsaka, the Kyōto branch has the advantage of a stunning location beside the Oi-gawa, nestled at the foothills of Arashiyama. Here you can experience the full sensory delight of formal kaiseki cuisine. Only the finest ingredients are used, prepared by master chefs and served in exquisite antique porcelain ware on priceless lacquered trays—all in an elegant private room sparsely decorated with a hanging scroll painted by a famous master, whose message sets the seasonal theme for the evening. The ability to identify the vessels used, an appreciation of the literary allusions made in the combination of objects and foods served, and knowledge of the arts of Japan all add depth to the experience. Expect to spend a minimum of two hours here. Kitcho closes for dinner at 7. *58 Susuki-no-bamba-chō, Tenryū-ji, Saga, Ukyō-ku, tel. 075/881–1101. Reservations essential. Jacket and tie. AE, DC, MC, V. Closed Wed.*

$$–$$$ **NISHIKI.** Tucked behind a rustic bamboo fence, Nishiki sits on
★ an island in the middle of the Oi-gawa, surrounded by the densely forested Arashiyama mountains. The *oshukuzen-bentō* lunch is the best sampler of formal, Kyōto-style kaiseki cuisine, for the reasonable price of ¥3,800. Unlike most other bentō lunches, it is served in seven courses and is so beautifully presented in a tiered lacquer box, with meticulous attention to the finest seasonal ingredients, that it rivals other meals at three times the price. A summer lunch might include a course of *kamo-nasu*, the prized Kyōto eggplant, served *dengaku*-style—smothered in sweet miso sauce in a silver serving dish the shape of an eggplant. The top layer of the lacquer box might be covered with a miniature bamboo trellis in which are nestled tiny porcelain cups the shape of morning glories, a favorite summer flower in Kyōto, each one filled with a different appetizer—a touch of sea urchin or a few sprigs of spinach in sesame sauce. Nishiki is close to the Togetsu-kyō Bridge. Call for reservations or expect a 30-minute wait. The last dinner order is taken at 7:30. *Nakanoshima Kōen-guchi, Arashiyama, Ukyō-ku, tel. 075/871–8888. DC, MC, V. Closed Tues.*

$$ **SAGANO.** Amid Arashiyama's lush, green bamboo forests, this
★ quiet retreat serves one of the finest *yudōfu* meals—cubes of bean curd simmered in a broth at your table—in Kyōto. The full course includes such local delicacies as tempura and *aburage*

(deep-fried tofu) with black sesame seeds and a gingko-nut center garnished with a sprig of *kinome* leaves from the Japanese pepper tree. Take a seat at the sunken counter, and waitresses in kimonos will prepare the meal in front of you—with a backdrop of antique wood-block prints on folding screens, surrounded by walls lined with delicately hand-painted antique porcelain bowls—or walk out through the garden to private, Japanese-style rooms in the back. If weather permits, you can dine on low tables in the courtyard garden beneath towering bamboo. Reservations are a good idea year-round, and particularly during fall foliage season, when the maple trees of Arashiyama are stunning. Arrive before 5:30 for dinner in the tatami rooms, before 6:30 for counter service. *45 Susuki-no-bamba-chō, Saga, Tenryū-ji, Ukyō-ku, tel. 075/ 861–0277. No credit cards.*

Spanish

$$–$$$ **BODEGON.** A white-walled, tile-floored, wrought-iron, and blown-glass Spanish restaurant in Arashiyama is about as rare (and welcome) as decent paella in a neighborhood famous for its tofu. Bodegon sits unobtrusively along the main street that runs through the center of this scenic district, combining Spanish fare and wine with Kyōto hospitality. A wildly popular tourist area in daylight, Arashiyama rolls up its sidewalks after dark, so Bodegon is a good place to escape the crowds downtown in the evening after other places close. *1 Susuki-no-bamba-chō, Saga, Tenryū-ji, tel. 075/872–9652. MC, V. Closed Thurs.*

CENTRAL KYŌTO

Coffee Shops

$ ★ **HONYARADŌ.** This log cabin–like coffee shop, east of Doshisha University, is a "home away from dormitory" for students. Here you'll find what's left of the peace movement—environmentalists, poets, and musicians—eating their lunches. The notices on the bulletin board are of a less incendiary nature these days, but the sandwiches are still on homemade wheat bread, and the stew is still good. Bring a good book (this guide, perhaps?), order some food, and relax. *Imadegawa-dōri, Tera-machi Nishi-Iru, Kamigyō-ku, tel. 075/222–1574. Reservations not accepted. No credit cards.*

$ **INODA.** Hidden down a side street in the center of town, this century-old establishment is one of Kyōto's oldest and best-loved *kissaten* (coffee shops). The turn-of-the-20th-century, Western-style brick buildings along Sanjō-dōri nearby are part of a historic preservation district, and Inoda's original old-shop blends well with its surroundings. Floor-to-ceiling glass windows overlook an interior garden, and the place even has some stained-glass windows and a pair of witty parrots. The coffee is excellent, to boot, for breakfast, lunch, or a break from sightseeing. Inoda closes at 6 PM. *Sakai-machi-dōri, Sanjō-sagaru, Nakagyō-ku, tel. 075/221–0507. Reservations not accepted. No credit cards.*

$ **STARBUCKS.** Yes, the rumor is true. Kyōto welcomed its first branch of "McCoffee" in June 1999. If you're pining for a cup of stronger-than-it-should-be brew, just head to Shijō-dōri near the Karasuma subway station, east of the Daimaru department store. *Yasaka Shijō Bldg., Tachi-uri Nakano machi 106, Shijō-dōri, Yanaginobaba Nishi-Iru, tel. 075/231–5008. MC, V.*

French

$$$ **NATSUKA.** This fine French restaurant with a reasonably priced
★ lunch menu overlooks the Kamo-gawa. The Japanese couple who manage the place lived and learned their trade in Paris. The dessert tray here is sumptuous, with a choice of two freshly baked delights from about eight possibilities. The last order must go in by 8. *Ponto-chō, Shijō-agaru, Higashi-gawa, Nakagyō-ku, tel. 075/ 255–2105. MC. Closed Wed.*

$$$ **OGAWA.** Down a narrow passageway across from the Takase-gawa
★ is the place to taste the best in Kyōto-style nouvelle cuisine.

Finding a seat at the counter of this intimate French restaurant is like getting tickets for opening night at the opera—one you've never seen. With particularly Japanese sensitivity to the best ingredients only in the peak of the season, proprietor Ogawa promises never to bore by serving the same meal twice. *Ayu*, a popular local river fish, is served in summer, salmon in fall, crab in winter, shrimp in spring. Ogawa prepares marvelous sauces and puddings—even fresh papaya sherbet and mango mousse with mint sauce. The full-course meal at lunch and dinner is spectacular, but some prefer to order hors d'oeuvres with wine. Counter seating is available for only 16. *Kiya-machi Oike-agaru Higashi-Iru, Nakagyō-ku, tel. 075/256–2203. Reservations essential. Jacket and tie. AE, DC, MC, V. Closed Tues.*

Indian

$–$$ ASHOKA. Kyōto, although more famous for its fine Japanese restaurants, has begun to look to the rest of the world for dining options. One of the first such international restaurants to open its doors in the capital of culinary daintiness was Ashoka. The dazzling *Thali* course dinner (about 10 small plates) consists of half a dozen curries in small bowls on a brass tray with rice and tandoori dishes—order this only if you're very hungry. Red carpets, carved screens, brass lanterns, and tuxedoed waiters set the mood, and diners wear everything from denim to silk. The last food order is at 9 PM, 8:30 PM on Sunday. *Kikusui Bldg., 3rd floor, Tera-machi-dōri, Shijō-agaru, Nakagyō-ku, tel. 075/241–1318. AE, DC, MC, V. Closed 2nd Tues. of month.*

Italian

$$$ **DIVO-DIVA.** As Japan enjoys an Italian food boom, divo-diva continues to set the standard in Kyōto. Its 31 seats are usually all occupied, often with weary Daimaru shoppers. The chefs here have all trained in Italy, and the fare is authentic Italian but with a

Japanese flair for color and design. The wine list is interesting and the pasta and breads are homemade. Lunch sets are an especially good value. Tasteful lighting sets off the contemporary decor. *Nishiki-kōji, Takakura-Nishi-Iru, Nakagyō-ku, tel. 075/256–1326. AE, DC, MC, V. Closed Wed. and 2nd and 3rd Tues. of month.*

$$ CUCINA IL VIALE. ★ The house speciality is not green eggs and ham, but Dr. Seuss would be thrilled nonetheless by the electric-pink tomato sauce served over handmade pasta at Cucina Il Viale. This Italian restaurant a few blocks from Nijō-jō dishes up pasta and fresh seasonal vegetables at a comfortable wooden counter or tables. The two chef-owners are usually quite busy behind the counter preparing the day's menu, but if they have time they may show you how the pasta is made. Courses A and B include antipasti; pasta topped with the house specialty, a pink sauce made from pureed sweet tomatoes; dessert; and espresso. Course B also comes with a fish or meat dish, which changes periodically and is always an authentic Italian creation with a twist. Enjoy a glass of extremely spicy ginger ale while you watch the chef weigh out your pasta and prepare the meal. The light mousse and litchi dessert alone is worth the visit. *Horikawa, Oike Nishi-iru, Nakagyō-ku, tel. 075/812–2366. AE, V. Closed Mon. No lunch Tues.*

$ CAPRICCIOSA. ★ Simple decor in striking colors and huge bowls of steaming spaghetti make this unpretentious Italian restaurant, part of a nationwide chain, a popular venue. The pasta dishes are large enough to share, and the pizzas are a good value. Lovers of Italian food may take issue with what is essentially a poor imitation of the real thing, but those looking for a cheap feed before boarding the Shinkansen (the restaurant is conveniently located under Kyōto Eki) won't be disappointed. Capricciosa has two more branches, on Kawara-machi-dōri in the Opa department store and in the Vox building. *Kyōto Eki basement, Porta Restaurant Zone, tel. 075/343–3499, www.capricciosa.com. No credit cards. Closed 3rd Tues. of month.*

Japanese

$$$$ MANKAMERO. Established in 1716, Mankamero is the only restaurant in Kyōto that offers formal *yusoku ryōri*, the type of cuisine once served to members of the imperial court. A specially appointed imperial chef prepares the food, using utensils made only for this type of cuisine. Dressed in ceremonial robes, the chef "dismembers" the fish and elaborately arranges its sections to have them brought to you on pedestal trays. Prices are also quite elaborate—up to ¥30,000 per person for the full yusoku ryōri repertoire—though in recent years an incomparable *take-kago bentō* lunch (served in a bamboo basket) has been within reach of wealthy commoners at ¥6,000. Mankamero is on the west side of Inokuma-dōri north of Demizu-dōri. It closes at 8 PM. *Inokuma-dōri, Demizu-agaru, Kamigyō-ku, tel. 075/441–5020. Reservations essential. Jacket and tie. AE, DC, MC, V. Closed once a month.*

$$$–$$$$ EBISUGAWA-TEI. Housed in a Meiji-era villa of former industrialist Baron Fujita are two excellent steak restaurants, both serving the celebrated beer-fed and massaged Ōmi beef. The more expensive and more formal **Ōmi** serves slightly higher-quality beef (men should wear jacket and tie). The **Chidori** is a bit less formal but also serves superb beef and has a better view of the garden. You can stop in at the bar in the basement of the Fujita Hotel for a drink beside the beautiful duck pond and waterfall. *Fujita Hotel, Nijō-dōri, Kiya-machi Kado, Nakagyō-ku, tel. 075/222–1511. AE, DC, MC, V.*

$$–$$$$ YOSHIKAWA. This quiet, traditional inn with landscaped gardens is within walking distance of the downtown shopping area. The specialty of the house is tempura, either a full-course dinner served in a tatami room or a lunch at the counter in its cozy "tempura corner," where the chef fries each vegetable and shrimp in front of you while you wait. Tempura should be light and crisp— best right from the pot—and for this Yoshikawa is famous. English is spoken. Yoshikawa closes at 8:30. *Tomino-kōji, Oike-sagaru,*

Nakagyō-ku, tel. 075/221–5544 or 075/221–0052. Jacket and tie at dinner. AE, DC, MC, V. Closed Sun.

$$$ MISHIMA-TEI. This is really the one choice for sukiyaki in Kyōto. In the heart of the downtown shopping district, it is also one of the best restaurants in the area. Kyōto housewives line up out front to pay premium prices for Mishima-tei's high-quality beef, sold by the 100-gram over the counter at the meat shop downstairs. Mishima-tei was established in 1904, and climbing the staircase of this traditional wood-frame restaurant with its turn-of-the-20th-century atmosphere is like journeying into the past. Down the long, dark corridors, with polished wood floors, kimono-clad servers bustle about with trays of beef and refills of sake to dozens of private tatami-mat rooms. Ask for a room that faces the central courtyard garden for the best view. Plan on dining by 7, as the service—and the preparation of your food—can be rushed toward the end of the evening. Tera-machi, Sanjō-sagaru, Higashi-Iru, Nakagyō-ku, tel. 075/221–0003. AE, DC, MC, V. Closed Wed.

$$ ŌIWA. Ōiwa, which is at the head of the Takase-gawa (canal), south of the Fujita Hotel, serves kushikatsu, skewered meats and vegetables battered, deep-fried, and then dipped in a variety of sauces. The building itself is actually a kura (treasure house) that belonged to a kimono merchant family, and it's one of the first to have been turned into a restaurant in Kyōto, where restorations of this type are still a relatively new idea. The Japanese chef trained in one of the finest French restaurants in Tōkyō, and his version of kushikatsu (usually considered a working man's snack with beer) has an unpretentious elegance. Order by the skewer or ask for the omakase set course. Ōiwa is a fine place to spend a relaxing evening. Kiya-machi-dōri, Nijō-sagaru, Nakagyō-ku, tel. 075/231–7667. No credit cards. Closed Wed.

$$ SHINSEN-EN HEIHACHI. Imagine munching on a foot-long hot dog while gazing upon the Rose Garden at the White House. You'll be doing the Japanese equivalent of this when you order a pot-for-two of Japan's fattest udon noodles and view all that remains of the once extensive garden of Kyōto's first imperial palace. When Emperor Kammu established Heian-kyō in 794, he built a pleasure garden within the main enclosure of the new capital's first Imperial Palace. The 33-acre Sacred Spring Garden contained pleasure pavilions for moon-viewing, fishing, and waterfall-viewing as well as pavilions for dance, sumō wrestling, and poetry contests. Today all that remains of the garden's original Chinese design is a garden pond with a brilliant red bridge. Occupying the land, now owned by the Tōji temple, is a restaurant famous in southwestern Japan for its extremely fat udon noodles. You can also sample the kaiseki ryōri here while viewing the elegant reminder of Heian-kyō's glorious past. The northern entrance of the restaurant faces the southern wall of Nijō-jō. *Nijō-jō Minami-gawa, Nakagyō-ku, tel. 075/841–0811. AE, MC, V.*

$–$$ AGATHA. This restaurant offers a "mystery" twist on the *robatayaki* (charcoal grill). The decor is period Agatha Christie—'40s book covers and movie posters, polished marble walls, potted palms, decent jazz, black-and-white-checkerboard floors. Watch the chef grill interesting variations on traditional delicacies, such as white, long-stem enoki mushrooms wrapped in strips of thinly sliced beef, scallops in bacon, or pork in *shiso* (a mintlike leaf). Both the A course and the B course combine these treats with unadorned standards such as *tebasaki* (grilled chicken wings). Salad and appetizers are included, and a wide selection of drinks are available—everything from sake to a gin fizz. Popular with the *juppie* (Japanese yuppie) crowd, this restaurant has two other branches in Kyōto, and one each in Ōsaka and Tōkyō. *Yurika Bldg., 2nd floor, Kiya-machi-dōri, Sanjō-agaru, Nakagyō-ku, tel. 075/223–2379. AE, DC, MC, V. No lunch.*

$–$$ TAGOTO. One of the best noodle shops in the downtown area has been serving soup with homemade *soba* (buckwheat noodles) for more than a hundred years in the same location on a shopping street that is now almost completely modernized. Tagoto, too, has remodeled, and the result is a pleasant surprise—modern yet in traditional Japanese style, with natural woods, shōji (rice-paper) windows, tatami mats, and an interior garden integrated with slate floors and the comfort of air-conditioning. Tagoto serves both thin soba and thick white udon noodle dishes with a variety of ingredients, such as shrimp tempura, hot or cold to suit the season. It's on the north side of the covered Sanjō Arcade, half a block west of Kawaramachi-dōri. *Sanjō-dōri, Tera-machi Higashi-Iru, Nakagyō-ku, tel. 075/ 221–3030. Reservations not accepted. AE, DC, MC, V.*

$ **DAIKOKUYA.** If you're shopping downtown and want a quick meal, stop in at Daikokuya for a soba dish or *domburi*, a bowl of rice with your choice of toppings. The *oyako domburi*, rice with egg and chicken, is the best choice (*oyako* means "parent and child"). The buckwheat for the soba is ground in-house on an antique stone mill powered by a wooden waterwheel. Fresh noodles are also served with exceedingly delicate tempura. Both tatami and table-and-chair seating are available. You can recognize Daikokuya by its red lantern and water mill. *281 Minami-kurumaya chō, Takoyakushi, Kiya-machi Nishi-Iru, Nakagyō-ku, tel. 075/221–2818. Reservations not accepted. AE, D, MC, V. Closed Tues.*

Thai

$$–$$$ **E-SAN.** Sitting at tables decorated with elephant carvings in a restaurant where spicy food and Thai karaoke are the order of the day, you might be convinced you're a million miles from Kyōto's Imperial Palace; in fact, you're only a stone's throw away. E-san's popular lunch buffet is filling and a good value at ¥1,200; dinner prices start at ¥6,000. If the food is too hot for your taste, order a bowl of delicious sweet-potato ice cream to cool down. *Imadegawa-dōri, Kamigyō-ku, tel. 075/441–6199. MC, V.*

NORTHERN KYŌTO

To get to restaurants in northern Kyōto, take the Eizan Electric Railway on the Kurama Line to Shūgaku-in Eki; then proceed by taxi.

Japanese

$$$–$$$$ ★ **HEIHACHI-JAYA.** A bit off the beaten path in the northeastern corner of Kyōto, along the old road to the Sea of Japan, this roadside inn has provided comfort to many a weary traveler during its 400-year history. Heihachi-Jaya hugs the levee of the Takano-gawa and is surrounded by maple trees in a quiet garden with a stream. Apart from the excellent *mugitoro* bentō lunch— which includes, among other dishes, grated mountain-potato salad served with barley rice—and the full-course kaiseki dinner, what makes this restaurant special is its clay sauna, the *kamaburo*, a mound-shape clay steam bath heated from beneath the floor by a pinewood fire. Have a bath and sauna, change into a cotton kimono if you wish, and retire to the dining room (or to a private room) for a *very* relaxing meal—an experience not to be missed. Heihachi-Jaya closes at 9 PM. *8–1 Kawagishi-chō, Yamabana, Sakyō-ku, tel. 075/781–5008. AE, DC, MC, V.*

$$$–$$$$ ★ **SAGENTA.** Discovering the town of Kibune is one of the best parts of summer in Kyōto. A short bump-and-rumble train ride into the mountains north of Kyōto on the nostalgic little Keifuku train leaves you on a mountain path that leads farther up into the forest beside a cool stream. The path is lined with restaurants that place tables near the stream in summer, when you can dine beneath a canopy of trees, with the water flowing at your feet. Sagenta is the last of these restaurants, at the very top of the slope, and it serves kaiseki lunches year-round, as well as one-pot *nabe* (stew) dishes in fall and winter. It's reasonably priced, particularly for its popular summertime specialty, *nagashi-somen*, chilled noodles that flow down a bamboo spout from the kitchen to a boat-shape trough; you catch the noodles from the trough as they float past, dip them in a sauce, and eat them with mushrooms, seasonal green vegetables, and shrimp. Reservations are advised in summer. To get here take the Eizan Electric Railway on the Kurama Line to Kibuneguchi Eki and then transfer to the Keifuku train to Kibune. Allow a good 45 minutes from central Kyōto. *76*

Kibune-chō, Kurama, Sakyō-ku, tel. 075/741–2244. AE, DC, MC, V. Closed periodically in winter.

$–$$$ AZEKURA. ★ On the northern outskirts of Kyōto, not far from Kamigamo Jinja, Azekura serves home-style buckwheat noodles under the giant wooden beams of a 300-year-old sake warehouse. Originally built in Nara, the warehouse was moved here more than 25 years ago by kimono merchant Mikio Ichida, who also maintains a textile exhibition hall, a small museum, and a weavers' workshop within the walls of this former samurai estate. Have lunch on low stools around a small charcoal brazier or on tatami next to a window overlooking the garden and waterwheel outside. The soba noodles at Azekura have a heartier country flavor than you'll find in most of the other noodle shops in town. This is a perfect place to stop while exploring the Shake-machi district around the shrine, an area in which priests and farmers have lived for more than 10 centuries. Azekura closes at 5 PM. *30 Okamoto-chō, Kamigamo, Kita-ku, tel. 075/701–0161. Reservations not accepted. No credit cards. Closed Mon.*

$$ IZUSEN. In the garden of Daiji-in, a subtemple of Daitoku-ji, this restaurant specializes in shōjin ryōri, vegetarian Zen cuisine. Lunches are presented in sets of red-lacquer bowls of diminishing sizes, each one fitting inside the next when the meal is completed. Two Kyōto specialties, *fu* (glutinous wheat cake) and *yuba* (curd from steamed soy milk), are served in a multitude of inventive forms—in soups and sauces that prove vegetarian cuisine to be as exciting as any meat dish. You can dine in tatami-mat rooms, and in warm weather at low tables outside in the temple garden. Reservations are recommended in spring and fall. Izusen closes at 4 PM. *4 Daitoku-ji-chō, Murasakino, Kita-ku, tel. 075/491–6665. No credit cards. Closed Thurs.*

In This Chapter

Updated by Lauren Sheridan

shopping

DESPITE THE HIGH PRICE of many goods, shopping is one of the great
pleasures of a trip to Kyōto. The crafts you will find in Kyōto are,
for their superb artistry and refinement, among the world's finest.
The city is especially known for its fine dolls, fans, ceramics,
laquerware, and silk. Color, balance of form, and absolutely
superb craftsmanship make these items exquisite and well worth
the price you'll pay.

Most shops slide open their doors at 10, and many shopkeepers
partake of the morning ritual of sweeping and watering the
entrance to welcome the morning's first customers. Shops lock
up at 6 or 7 in the evening. Stores often close sporadically once
or twice a month, so it's a good idea to call in advance if you're
making a special trip. As Sunday is a big shopping day for the
Japanese, most stores remain open.

The traditional greeting of a shopkeeper to a customer is *o-
ideyasu* (Kyōto-ben, the Kyōto dialect for "honored to have you
here"), voiced in a lilting Kyōto dialect with the required bowing
of the head. When a customer makes a purchase, the
shopkeeper will respond with *o-okini* ("thank you" in Kyōto-
ben), a smile, and a bow. Take notice of the careful effort and
adroitness with which purchases are wrapped; it's an art in
itself. Also, you'll still hear the clicking of an abacus, rather than
the crunching of a cash register, in many Kyōto shops. American
Express, MasterCard, Visa, and traveler's checks are widely
accepted.

If you plan to make shopping one of your prime pursuits in Kyōto, look for a copy of Diane Durston's thorough *Old Kyōto: A Guide to Traditional Shops, Restaurants, and Inns.*

SHOPPING DISTRICTS

Compared with sprawling Tōkyō, Kyōto is compact and relatively easy to navigate. Major shops line both sides of **SHIJŌ-DŌRI,** which runs east–west, and **KAWARA-MACHI-DŌRI,** which runs north–south. Concentrate on Shijō-dōri between Yasaka Jinja and Karasuma Eki as well as Kawara-machi-dōri between Sanjō-dōri and Shijō-dōri. Nearby **KIYA-MACHI-DŌRI,** famous for its watering holes, has expensive fashion outlets, like that of Paul Smith and other European designers.

Some of modern Kyōto's shopping districts are to be found underground. **PORTA,** under Kyōto Eki, hosts more than 200 shops and restaurants in a sprawling, subterranean arcade. **ZEST OIKE,** which is newer than Porta, is accessible from the Kyōto Shiyakusho-Mae subway station.

ROADS LEADING TO KIYOMIZU-DERA are steep inclines, yet you may hardly notice the steepness for all of the alluring shops that line the way to the temple. Be sure to peek in for unique gifts. Food shops offer sample morsels, and tea shops serve complimentary cups of tea.

SHIN-KYŌGOKU, a covered arcade running parallel to Kawara-machi-dōri, is another general-purpose shopping area with many souvenir shops.

CRAFTS CENTERS

The **KYŌTO CRAFT CENTER,** on Shijō-dōri in Gion, has two floors of contemporary and traditional crafts for sale in a modern setting. More than 100 crafts studios are represented, giving a diversity to the products for sale. *Shijō-dōri, Gion-machi, Higashiyama-ku, tel.* 075/561–9660. *Thurs.–Tues.* 11–7.

The **KYŌTO HANDICRAFT CENTER,** a seven-story shopping emporium, sells everything from tape decks and pearl necklaces to porcelain and lacquerware designed to appeal to tourists. It's a good place to compare prices and grab last-minute souvenirs. *Kumano Jinja Higashi, Sakyō-ku, tel. 075/761–5080. Feb.–Dec., daily 9:30–6; Jan., daily 9:30–5:30.*

DEPĀTO

Kyōto *depāto* (department stores) are small in comparison to their mammoth counterparts in Tōkyō and Ōsaka. They still, however, carry a wide range of goods and are great places for one-stop souvenir shopping. Wandering around the food halls (in all but Hankyū) is also a good way to build up an appetite. Note that all the stores close for a few days each month. You can call at the beginning of the month to find out about scheduled closures.

DAIMARU is conveniently located on the main Shijō-dori shopping avenue. Its basement food hall is the best in town. *Shijō-Karasuma, Shimogyō-ku, tel. 075/211–8111. Daily 10–7:30.*

HANKYŪ, directly across from Takashimaya on Kawara-machi-dōri, has two restaurant floors. Window displays show the type of food served, and prices are clearly marked. *Shijō-kawara-machi, Shimogyō-ku, tel. 075/223–2288. Daily 10–7:30.*

ISETAN, in the Kyōto Eki building, has 13 floors, including a restaurant floor, an amusement arcade, and an art gallery. It closes periodically on Tuesday. *Karasuma-dōri, Shimogyō-ku, tel. 075/352–1111. Daily 10–7:30.*

KINTETSU is on Karasuma-dōri, the avenue leading north from Kyōto Eki. *Karasuma-dōri, Shimogyō-ku, tel. 075/361–1111. Daily 10–7:30.*

TAKASHIMAYA, on Kawara-machi-dōri, has a well-trained English-speaking staff at its information desk, as well as a convenient money-exchange counter on its premises. *Shijō-kawara-machi, Shimogyō-ku, tel. 075/221–8811. Daily 10–7:30.*

FOOD AND TEMPLE MARKETS

Kyōto has a wonderful food market, **NISHIKI-KŌJI,** which branches off from the Shin-Kyōgoku covered arcade across from the Daimaru department store in central Kyōto. Look for delicious grilled fish dipped in soy for a tasty snack. Try to avoid the market in late afternoon, when housewives come to do their daily shopping. The market is long and narrow; in a sizable crowd there's always the possibility of being pushed into the display of fresh fish.

Several **TEMPLE MARKETS** take place in Kyōto each month. These are great places to pick up bargain kimonos or unusual souvenirs. They're also some of the best spots for people-watching. The largest and most famous is the market at **TŌ-JI,** which takes place on the 21st of each month. The temple also hosts a smaller market devoted to antiques on the first Sunday of the month. The market at **KITANO TENMAN-GŪ** is held on the 25th of each month. A market specializing in homemade goods is held at **CHION-JI** on the 15th. To get to the Chion-ji market, take Bus 206 from Kyōto Eki to Hyakumanben.

TRADITIONAL ITEMS AND GIFT IDEAS

Art and Antiques

NAWATE-DŌRI between Shijō-dōri and Sanjō-dōri is noted for fine antique textiles, ceramics, and paintings.

SHINMONZEN-DŌRI holds the key to shopping for art and antiques in Kyōto. It's an unpretentious little street of two-story wooden buildings that is lined with telephone and electricity poles between Higashi-ōji-dōri and Hanami-kōji-dōri, just north of Gion. What gives the street away as a treasure trove are the large credit-card signs jutting out from the shops. There are no fewer than 17 shops specializing in scrolls, *netsuke* (small carved figures to attach to Japanese clothing), lacquerware, bronze, wood-block prints, paintings, and antiques. Shop with confidence, because shopkeepers are trustworthy and goods are authentic. Pick up a copy of the pamphlet *Shinmonzen Street Shopping Guide* from your hotel or from the Tourist Information Center.

TERA-MACHI-DŌRI between Oike-dōri and Maruta-machi is known for antiques of all kinds and tea-ceremony utensils.

Bamboo

The Japanese wish their sons and daughters to be as strong and flexible as bamboo. Around many Japanese houses are small bamboo groves, for the deep-rooted plant withstands earthquakes. On the other hand, bamboo is so flexible it bends into innumerable shapes. Bamboo groves surround the entire city of Kyōto. The wood is carefully cut and dried for several months before being stripped and woven into baskets and vases.

KAGOSHIN has been making bamboo baskets since 1862. Only the best varieties of bamboo are used in this fiercely proud little shop. *Ōhashi-higashi, Sanjō-dōri, Higashiyama-ku, tel. 075/771–0209. Mon.–Sat. 9–6.*

Ceramics

ASAHI-DO, in the heart of the pottery district near Kiyomizu-dera, specializes in Kyōto-style hand-painted porcelain. *1–280 Kiyomizu, Higashiyama-ku, tel. 075/531–2181. Daily 9–6.*

TACHIKICHI, on Shijō-dōri west of Kawara-machi, has contemporary and traditional wares and the best reputation in town. *Shijō-Tominokōji, Nakagyō-ku, tel. 075/211–3143. Thurs.–Tues. 10–7.*

Dolls

Ningyō were first used in Japan in the purification rites associated with the Doll Festival, an annual family-oriented event on March 3. Kyōto ningyō are made with fine detail and embellishment.

NAKANISHI TOKU SHŌTEN has old museum-quality dolls. The owner, Mr. Nakanishi, turned his extensive doll collection into the shop two decades ago and has since been educating customers with his vast knowledge of the doll trade. *359 Moto-chō, Yamato-ōji Higashi-Iru, Furumonzen-dōri, Higashiyama-ku, tel. 075/561–7309. Daily 10–5.*

Folk Crafts

For many the prize souvenir of a visit to Kyōto is the *shuinshu*, a booklet usually no larger than 4 by 6 inches. It's most often covered with brocade, and the blank sheets of heavyweight paper inside continuously fold out. You can find them at stationery stores or at temples for as little as ¥1,000 and use them as "passports" to collect ink stamps from places you visit while in Japan. Stamps and stamp pads are ubiquitous in Japan—at sights, train stations, and some restaurants. Most ink stamping will be done for free; at temples monks will write calligraphy over the stamp for a small fee.

KURAYA HASHIMOTO has one of the best collections of antique and newly forged swords. *Nishihorikawa-dōri, Oike-agaru (southeast corner of Nijō-jō), Nakagyō-ku, tel. 075/821–2791. Daily 10–6.*

.At **RYUSHIDO** you can stock up on calligraphy and *sumi* supplies, including writing brushes, ink sticks, ink stones, paper, paperweights, and water stoppers. *Nijō-agaru, Tera-machi-dōri (north of Nijō), Kamigyō-ku, tel. 075/252–4120. Daily 10–6.*

YAMATO MINGEI-TEN, next to the Maruzen Bookstore downtown, has the best selection of folk crafts, including ceramics, metalwork, paper, lacquerware, and textiles. *Kawara-machi, Takoyakushi-agaru, Nakagyō-ku, tel. 075/221–2641. Wed.–Mon. 10–8:30.*

Kimonos and Accessories

Shimmering new silk kimonos can cost more than ¥1,000,000—they are art objects, as well as couture—while equally stunning old silk kimonos can cost less than ¥3,000. You can find used kimonos at some local end-of-the-month temple markets.

AIZEN KOBO, two blocks east of the textile center on Imadegawa-dōri and a block south, specializes in the finest handwoven indigo-dyed textiles. The shop is in a traditional weaving family's home, and the friendly owners will show you a wide variety of dyed and woven goods, including garments designed by Hisako Utsuki, the owner's wife. *Ōmiya Nishi-Iru, Nakasuji-dōri, Kamigyō-ku, tel. 075/441–0355. Mon.–Sat. 9–5:30.*

JŪSAN-YA has been selling *tsugekushi* (boxwood combs) for more than 60 years. *Kanzashi*, the hair ornaments worn with kimonos, are also available. *Shinkyōgoku Higashi-Iru, Shijō-dōri, Shimogyō-ku, tel. 075/221–2008. Daily 10–6.*

Umbrellas protect kimonos from the scorching sun or pelting rain. Head for **KASAGEN** to purchase authentic oiled-paper umbrellas. The shop has been around since 1861, and its umbrellas are guaranteed to last years. *284 Gion-machi, Kita-gawa, Higashiyama-ku, tel. 075/561–2832. Daily 10–9.*

Beyond T-Shirts and Key Chains

BUDGET FOR A MAJOR PURCHASE If souvenirs are all about keeping the memories alive in the long haul, plan ahead to shop for something really special—a work of art, a rug or something else hand-crafted, or a major accessory for your home. One major purchase will stay with you far longer than a dozen tourist trinkets, and you'll have all the wonderful memories associated with shopping for it besides.

ADD TO YOUR COLLECTION Whether antiques, used books, salt and pepper shakers, or ceramic frogs are your thing, start looking in the first day or two. Chances are you'll want to scout around and then go back to some of the first shops you visited before you hand over your credit card.

GET GUARANTEES IN WRITING Is the vendor making promises? Ask him to put them in writing.

ANTICIPATE A SHOPPING SPREE If you think you might buy breakables, include a length of bubble wrap. Pack a large tote bag in your suitcase in case you need extra space. Don't fill your suitcase to bursting before you leave home. Or include some old clothing that you can leave behind to make room for new acquisitions.

KNOW BEFORE YOU GO Study prices at home on items you might consider buying while you're away. Otherwise you won't recognize a bargain when you see one.

PLASTIC, PLEASE Especially if your purchase is pricey and you're looking for authenticity, it's always smart to pay with a credit card. If a problem arises later on and the merchant can't or won't resolve it, the credit-card company may help you out.

The most famous fan shop in all of Kyōto is **MIYAWAKI BAISEN-AN,** in business since 1823. It delights customers not only with its fine collection of lacquered, scented, painted, and paper fans but also with the old-world atmosphere that emanates from the building that houses the shop. *Tominokōji Nishi-Iru, Rokkaku-dōri, Nakagyō-ku, tel. 075/221–0181. Daily 9–6.*

The **NISHIJIN ORIMONO** (Textile Center), in the Japanese silk weaving district of Nishijin, provides an orientation on silk-weaving techniques. *Horikawa-dōri, Imadegawa-Minami-Iru, Kamigyō-ku, tel. 075/451–9231. Free. Daily 9–5.*

Visit **TAKUMI** for kimono accessories like obis, handbags, and furoshiki (gift-wrapping cloth). *Sanjō-sagaru, Kawara-machi-dōri, Nakagyō-ku, tel. 075/221–2278. Daily 10:30–9.*

In This Chapter

Updated by Lauren Sheridan

nightlife and the arts

KYOTO IS QUICKLY FOLLOWING TŌKYŌ AND ŌSAKA on domestic and international performing artists' circuits. The city has hosted the likes of Bruce Springsteen, but it's better known for its traditional performances—dance and Kabuki and Nō theater. All dialogue at theaters is in Japanese, of course.

Information on performances is available from a number of sources; the most convenient is your hotel concierge or guest-relations manager, who may even have a few tickets on hand, so don't hesitate to ask. For further information on Kyōto's arts scene check the music and theater sections of the monthly magazine **Kansai Time Out,** available at bookshops for ¥300; you can also find information on the Web site (www.kto.co.jp). Another source is the **Kyōto Visitor's Guide,** which devotes a few pages to "This Month's Theater." It's available free from JNTO's Tourist Information Center (TIC), directly across from Kyōto Eki. It's strongly suggested that you stop by the TIC if you're interested in the performing arts in Kyōto, but if you don't have time to visit in person, you can call and speak with an English-speaking information officer.

Though Kyōto's nightlife is more sedate than Ōsaka's, the areas around the old geisha quarters downtown still thrive with nightclubs and bars. The Kiya-machi area along the small canal near Ponto-chō is as close to a consolidated nightlife area as you'll get in Kyōto. It's full of small watering holes with red lanterns (indicating inexpensive places) or small neon signs in front. It is also fun to walk around the Gion and Ponto-chō areas to try to catch a glimpse of a geisha or maiko (apprentice geisha) stealing down an alleyway on her way to or from an appointment.

THE ARTS

Gion Corner

Some call it a tourist trap, but for others it's a comprehensive introduction to Japanese performing arts. The one-hour show combines court music and dance, ancient comic plays, Kyōto-style dance performed by maiko, and puppet drama. Segments are also offered on tea ceremony, flower arrangement, and koto music.

Before attending a show, walk around Gion and Ponto-chō. You're likely to see beautifully dressed geisha and maiko making their way to work. It's permissible to take their picture—"Shashin o totte mō ii desu ka?" is the polite way to ask—but as they have strict appointments, don't delay them.

For tickets to Gion Corner, contact your hotel concierge or call the theater directly (Yasaka Hall, 1st floor, Gion, tel. 075/561–1119). The show costs ¥2,800—a bargain considering that it would usually cost 10 times as much to watch maiko and geisha perform. Two performances are held nightly at 7:40 and 8:40 March–November. No performances are offered August 16.

An even less expensive introduction to geisha arts can be had at the **INTERNATIONAL HOTEL KYŌTO** (Horikawa, Nijō-jō-mae, tel. 075/222–1111), which has free maiko dance performances in its first-floor lounge every evening 7:20–7:40. The hotel is opposite Nijō-jō.

Seasonal Dances

In the **MIYAKO ODORI**, in April, and the **KAMO-GAWA ODORI**, in May and October, geisha and maiko dances and songs pay tribute to the seasonal splendor of spring and fall. The stage settings are spectacular.

Tickets to performances at the **GION KABURENJŌ THEATER** (Gion Hanami-kōji, Higashiyama-ku, tel. 075/561–1115) cost ¥1,900, ¥3,800, and ¥4,300. Tickets at the **PONTO-CHŌ KABURENJŌ THEATER** (Ponto-chō, Sanjō-sagaru, Nakagyō-ku, tel. 075/221–2025) range from ¥1,650 to ¥3,800.

Kabuki

Kabuki emerged as a popular form of entertainment by women dancing lewdly in the early 17th century; before long, it had been banned by the authorities as a threat to public order. Eventually it cleaned up its act, and by the latter half of the 18th century it had become Everyman's theater par excellence—especially among the townspeople of hustling, hustling Edo. Kabuki had music, dance, and spectacle; it had acrobatics and sword fights; it had pathos and tragedy and historical romance and social satire. It no longer had bawdy beauties, however—women have been banned from the Kabuki stage since 1629—but in recompense it developed a professional role for female impersonators, who train for years to project a seductive, dazzling femininity. It had—and still has—superstars and quick-change artists and legions of fans, who bring their lunch to the theater, stay all day, and shout out the names of their favorite actors at the stirring moments in their favorite plays.

The traditions of Kabuki are passed down from generation to generation in a small group of families; the roles and great stage names are hereditary. The Kabuki repertoire does not really grow or change, but stars like Ennosuke Ichikawa and Tamasaburo Bando have put exciting, personal stamps on their performances that continue to draw audiences young and old.

Kabuki has found quite a following in the United States due to tours by Japanese Kabuki troupes in Washington, D.C., New

York, and a few other cities. Kabuki is faster paced than Nō, but a single performance can easily take half a day. Devoted followers pack *bentō* (box lunches) and sit patiently through the entire performance, mesmerized by each movement of the performers.

For a first-timer, however, the music and unique intonations of Kabuki might be a bit of an overload. Unless you're captured by the Kabuki spirit, don't spend more than an hour or two at Kyōto's famed **MINAMI-ZA** (Shijō Kamo-gawa, Higashiyama-ku, tel. 075/561–1155), the oldest theater in Japan. Beautifully renovated, it hosts a variety of performances year-round. Top Kabuki stars from around the country make guest appearances during the annual, monthlong **KAOMISE** (Face Showing) Kabuki Festival, in December. Ask at the Tourist Information Center for information. Tickets range from ¥2,000 to ¥9,000.

NŌ

Nō is a dramatic tradition far older than Kabuki; it reached a point of formal perfection in the 14th century and survives virtually unchanged from that period. Kabuki was Everyman's theater while Nō was developed for the most part under the patronage of the warrior class. It is dignified, ritualized, and symbolic. Many of the plays in the repertoire are drawn from classical literature or tales of the supernatural, and the texts are richly poetic. Some understanding of the plot of each play is necessary to enjoy a performance, which moves at a nearly glacial pace—the pace of ritual time—as it is solemnly chanted. The major Nō theaters often provide synopses of the plays in English.

While Kabuki actor is usually in brightly colored makeup derived from the Chinese opera, the principal character in a Nō play wears a carved wooden mask. Such is the skill of the actor—and the mysterious effect of the play—that the mask itself may appear expressionless until the actor "brings it to life," at which point the mask seems to express a considerable range of emotions. As in Kabuki, the various roles of the Nō repertoire all have specific costumes—robes of silk brocade with intricate patterns that are works of art in themselves. Nō is not a very *accessible* kind of theater: its language is archaic; its conventions are obscure; and its measured, stately pace can put even Japanese audiences to sleep.

Somewhat like Kabuki, Nō has a number of schools, the traditions of which developed as the exclusive property of hereditary families. Note that *kyōgen* are shorter, lighter plays that are often interspersed in between Nō performances and are much more accessible than Nō. Consider taking advantage of opportunities to see kyōgen rather than Nō.

Particularly memorable are outdoor performances of Nō, especially **TAKIGI NŌ,** held outdoors by firelight on the nights of June 1–2 in the precincts of the Heian Jingū. For more information about the performances, contact the Tourist Information Center.

Nō performances are held year-round and range from ¥4,000 to ¥6,000. **KANZE KAIKAN NŌ THEATER** (44 Enshōji-chō, Okazaki, Sakyō-ku, tel. 075/771–6114). **KONGO NŌ THEATER** (Muromachi, Shijō-agaru, Nakagyō-ku, tel. 075/221–3049).

NIGHTLIFE

Kyōto's only venue for acoustic, folk, and bluegrass is **CUP OF SUN** (west of junction of Shirakawa-dōri and Higashi-kurumaguchi-dōri, tel. 075/791–1001). Though only open on Saturday night from 8:30 to 11:00, **KENNY'S** (northwest corner of Shimei-dōri and Karasuma-dōri, tel. 075/415–1171) is a well-known country-and-western bar with live performances by one of Japan's C&W legends. Kenny has even played the Grand Ol' Opry in Nashville. **LE CLUB JAZZ** (Sanjo Arimoto Bldg., 2nd floor, Sanjō-Gokōmachi Nishi-Iru, tel. 075/211–5800) has jazz, blues, and soul gigs on Tuesday and sessions every night from

Not a Night Owl?

You can learn a lot about a place if you take its pulse after dark. So even if you're the original early-to-bed type, there's every reason to vary your routine when you're away from home.

EXPERIENCE THE FAMILIAR IN A NEW PLACE Whether your thing is going to the movies or going to concerts, it's always different away from home. In clubs, new faces and new sounds add up to a different scene. Or you may catch movies you'd never see at home.

TRY SOMETHING NEW Do something you've never done before. It's another way to dip into the local scene. A simple suggestion: Go out later than usual—go dancing late and finish up with breakfast at dawn.

EXPLORE A DAYTIME NEIGHBORHOOD AT NIGHT Take a nighttime walk through an explorable area you've already seen by day. You'll get a whole different view of it.

ASK AROUND If you strike up a conversation with like-minded people during the course of your day, ask them about their favorite spots. Your hotel concierge is another resource.

DON'T WING IT As soon as you've nailed down your travel dates, look into local publications or surf the Net to see what's on the calendar while you're in town. Look for hot regional acts, dance and theater, big-name performing artists, expositions, and sporting events. Then call or click to order tickets.

CHECK OUT THE NEIGHBORHOOD Whenever you don't know the neighborhood you'll be visiting, review safety issues with people in your hotel. What's the transportation situation? Can you walk there, or do you need a cab? Is there anything else you need to know?

CASH OR CREDIT? Know before you go. It's always fun to be surprised—but not when you can't cover your check.

Thursday to Monday. There's a ¥2,000 cover charge (including two drinks) on weekends. **LIVE SPOT RAG** (Kyōto Empire Bldg., 5th floor, Kiya-machi, tel. 075/241–0446), a jazz place north of Sanjō-dōri, has a reasonable cover charge of about ¥1,200 for its live sessions between 7 and 11. **MAMMA ZAPPA** (Takoyakushi-dōri, off Kawara-machi-dōri, south of Maruzen, tel. 075/255–4437) was David Bowie's choice of watering hole when he was in town. An arty crowd munches on Indonesian food while sipping cocktails. One of three Kansai-area **PIG & WHISTLE** pubs (across from Keihan Sanjō Eki, Shobi Bldg., 2nd floor, tel. 075/761–6022) is a popular hangout, and every weekend the Kyōto branch bulges at the seams.

One of the best clubs in Kansai is Kyōto's **METRO** (Ebisu Bldg., 2nd floor, Shimotsutsumi-chō 82, Maruta-machi Sagaru, Kawabata-dōri, Sakyō-ku, tel. 075/752–4765), which has an extremely wide range of regular events, from salsa to reggae, as well as frequent guest appearances by famous DJs from Tōkyō and abroad.

In This Chapter

Updated by Lauren Sheridan

where to stay

KYŌTO'S HOTEL ROOMS are often designed merely as places to rest at night. Most rooms are small by international standards, but they are adequate for relaxing after a busy day of sightseeing. As it is throughout Japan, service in this city is impeccable; the information desks are well stocked with maps and pamphlets about the sights. Assistant managers, concierges, and guest-relations managers are always available in the lobby to respond to your needs, although English may or may not be spoken.

Kyōto has Western- and Japanese-style accommodations, including traditional *ryokan*. Usually small, one- or two-story wooden structures with a garden or scenic view, ryokan provide traditional Japanese accommodations: simple rooms in which the bedding is rolled out onto the floor at night. Some ryokan have shared toilets and baths, so ask about these if you don't like to share facilities.

Do check out the listed Web sites. Many of the hotels offer heavily discounted rates in summer. You can often check room availability and reserve rooms on-line. Book at least a month in advance, or as early as three months ahead if you're traveling during peak spring and autumn seasons or around important Japanese holidays and festivals. Keep in mind the following festival dates when making reservations: May 15, July 16–17, August 16, and October 22. Rooms will be scarce at these times.

CATEGORY	COST*
$$$$	over ¥30,000
$$$	¥20,000–¥30,000
$$	¥8,000–¥20,000
$	under ¥8,000

*All prices are for a double room, excluding service and tax.

EASTERN KYŌTO

$$$–$$$$ MIYAKO HOTEL. The Miyako, the grande dame of Kyōto's Western-style hotels, has been around for more than a century. The hotel spreads across the hills of Kyōto, near the temples and shrines of the eastern district. Be sure to request a room with a view of the surrounding hills. Twenty Japanese-style rooms in two annexes have the feel of a traditional ryokan. *Sanjō-Keage, Higashiyama-ku, Kyōto-shi 605-0052, tel. 075/771–7111; 800/223–6800 in the U.S.; 0800/181–123 in the U.K.; fax 075/751–2490; www.miyakohotel.co.jp. 300 Western-style rooms, 20 Japanese-style rooms. 5 restaurants, 2 bars, coffee shop, pool, shops, meeting rooms. AE, DC, MC, V.*

$$$–$$$$ SEIKŌRŌ. ★ This lovely inn, established in 1831, is a short walk from busy Gojō Eki, a convenience that makes it popular among both gaijin and Japanese. A local resident who speaks English fluently manages the ryokan. Among the interesting decor are Western antiques that mysteriously blend in quite well with the otherwise traditional setting. When you return to Seikōrō after a day of sightseeing, you may get the distinct feeling that you're returning to your Japanese home. Breakfast and dinner are included. *Toiya-machi-dōri, Gojō-sagaru, Higashiyama-ku, Kyōto-shi 605-0907, tel. 075/561–0771, fax 075/541–5481. 23 Japanese-style rooms. AE, DC, MC, V.*

$$$–$$$$ YACHIYO. ★ Carefully shaped bushes, pine trees, and rocks surround the woodwork and low-hanging tiled eaves of the special entrance to this ryokan, and the sidewalk from the gate curves into the doorway. Yachiyo is less expensive than its brethren in the deluxe category but nevertheless provides fine, attentive care. Perhaps the biggest draw of the inn is its proximity to Nanzen-ji, one of the most appealing temples in Kyōto. You can reduce the cost of staying at this ryokan by choosing not to dine here. *34 Nanzen-ji-fukuchi-chō, Sakyō-ku, Kyōto-shi 606-8435, tel. 075/771–4148, fax 075/771–4140. 25 rooms, 20 with bath. AE, DC, MC, V.*

$$ HOLIDAY INN KYŌTO. With a bowling alley and an ice-skating rink, this member of the American chain has the best sports facilities of any hotel in Kyōto. The hotel is in a residential area with small, modern houses, occasionally interrupted by large, traditional estates. To compensate for its location away from most of the action, the hotel provides a shuttle bus to make the 30-minute run to and from Kyōto Eki every 90 minutes. The hotel is a 15-minute taxi ride from Kyōto's downtown area. *36 Nishihiraki-chō, Takano, Sakyō-ku, Kyōto-shi 606-8103, tel. 075/721–3131, fax 075/781–6178, www.holiday-inn.com. 270 rooms. 3 restaurants, 2 bars, coffee shop, indoor pool, sauna, driving range, tennis court, bowling, gym, ice-skating, shops. AE, DC, MC, V.*

$$ KYŌTO TRAVELER'S INN. This no-frills modern inn is in the perfect spot for sightseeing, with Heian Jingū, Nanzen-ji, and the museums in Okazaki Park just minutes away on foot. Its Western-style and Japanese-style rooms are plain and small but clean and practical; all have a private bath and toilet. Ask for a room with a view (most don't have one). Because of its location, size, and price, the hotel often hosts large travel groups. Head for the coffee shop on the first floor to look out over the river and plot your course for the day. In contrast to some of Kyōto's other budget inns, this one imposes no curfew. *Heian Jingū Torii-mae, Okazaki, Sakyō-ku, Kyōto-shi 606-8344, tel. 075/771–0225. 40 Western-style rooms, 38 Japanese-style rooms. Coffee shop, meeting room. AE, MC, V.*

$$ PENSION HIGASHIYAMA. A 10-minute walk from downtown and the major temples along the eastern foothills, this small pension overlooks the lovely Shira-kawa Canal, south of Sanjō-dōri. The pension has created a friendly atmosphere for families on a budget and is accustomed to gaijin. Several rooms have tatami, and all share bath. *474-23 Umemiya-chō, Shirakawa-suji, Sanjō-sagaru, Higashiyama-ku, Kyōto-shi 605-0061, tel. 075/882–1181. 15 rooms, 3 with toilet. Dining room. AE.*

$$ THREE SISTERS INN ANNEX (Rakutō-sōso Bekkan). A traditional inn popular with gaijin for decades, the annex—which is nicer than the main branch—sits on the northeast edge of Heian Jingū, down a trellised path that hides it from the street. This is a quiet and friendly place, and a good introduction to inn customs because the management is accustomed to foreign guests. On the down side, the rooms could use refurbishment, and the doors close at 11:30 PM sharp. *Heian Jingū, Higashi-kita-kado, Sakyō-ku, Kyōto-shi 606-8322, tel. 075/761–6333, fax 075/761–6335. 12 rooms. AE, DC.*

$–$$ RYOKAN YUHARA. Yuhara draws repeat visitors wishing to save a few yen while exploring Kyōto. The friendliness of the staff more than compensates for the spartan amenities. Especially rewarding is a springtime stay, when the cherry trees are in full bloom along the Takase-gawa, which the inn overlooks. This is a 15-minute walk from Gion and Ponto-chō. *188 Kagiya-chō, Shomen-agaru, Kiya-machi-dōri, Higashiyama-ku, Kyōto-shi 605-0909, tel. 075/371–9583. 8 Japanese-style rooms. No credit cards.*

WESTERN KYŌTO

$$$ SYŌENSŌ-HOSOGAWA-TEI. In the onsen (hot springs) village of Yunohana, set in the mountains of Tamba northwest of Kyōto, this hotel allows you to soak in your own rotemburo (outdoor bath) overlooking a private garden. If you're feeling adventurous you can get into the full swing of an onsen visit by joining other guests in one of the communal baths (separated by gender). The building itself looks like something out of the Twilight Zone, but the machiya (layers of sliding paper screens) facade of the lobby and the steps bordered on one side by a gently sloping waterfall suggest Old Kyōto. A kaiseki dinner is prepared with seasonal favorites, including Tamba boar in winter. Breakfast is also included in the room rate. An overnight stay at the hotel complements a trip to Arashiyama. For ¥600, you can take the scenic Sagano Torokko train, which leaves Saga Torokko station in Arashiyamas six minutes before the hour, for the 20-minute ride to Kameoka, where Yunohana is located. Call ahead to ask the hotel shuttle bus to meet you at the station. To return to Arashiyama, take the Hosogawa-kudari boat the next day. Alternatively, you can take the JR line between Kameoka and Kyōto stations. *Kameoka City, Yunohana-onsen, 621-0034, tel. 0771/22–0903, fax 0771/23–6572, www.syoenso.com. 56 Japanese-style rooms, 7 with bath. Restaurant, 2 lounges, hot springs, sauna, shops. AE, MC, V.*

$ UTANO YOUTH HOSTEL. If you like the onsen feel, without the onsen price, try the Utano, which provides a communal, indoor hot spring bath. Near Kinkaku-ji and Ryōan-ji, the hostel is convenient for sightseeing in Arashiyama and western Kyōto. Rooms, which have bunk beds, accommodate up to eight people. Sip tea or coffee with the other guests every night from 10 to 10:30. The friendly staff speaks English. Dinner and breakfast are served for a small additional fee. You can rent a bicycle here for ¥600 a day. Internet access is available. *29 Nakayama-cho, Uzumasa, Ukyō-ku Kyōto-shi 6160-8191, tel. 075/462–2288, fax 075/462–2289, web. kyoyo-inet.or.jp/org/utano-yh/. 25 rooms. Cafeteria, hot springs, tennis court, bicycles, coin laundry. AE, MC, V.*

CENTRAL KYŌTO

$$$$ HIIRAGIYA. For more than 150 years the Nishimura family has been ★ welcoming dignitaries and celebrities to this elegant inn. Founded in 1818 to accommodate provincial lords visiting the capital, the inn has welcomed Charlie Chaplin, Elizabeth Taylor, and Yukio Mishima in addition to its 19th-century samurai visitors. The inn is representative of Kyōto itself in the way it skillfully combines ancient and modern. Where else could you find cedar baths with chrome taps? And look out for the lacquered gourd designed by

kyōto lodging

ANA Hotel Kyōto, 7	Hotel Fujita Kyōto, 11	Miyako Hotel, 14	Syōensō-Hosogawa-tei, 3
Daimonjiya, 8	Kyōto Brighton Hotel, 5	New Miyako Hotel, 21	Takaraga-ike Prince Hotel, 1
Hiiragiya, 9		Pension Higashiyama, 16	Tawaraya, 10
Hiraiwa, 19	Kyōto Kokusai Hotel, 6	Rihga Royal Hotel Kyōto, 22	Three Sisters Inn Annex, 12
Hotel Granvia Kyōto, 20	Kyōto Tōkyū Hotel, 23	Ryokan Yuhara, 17	Utano Youth Hostel, 4
Holiday Inn Kyōto, 2	Kyōto Traveler's Inn, 15	Seikōrō, 18	Yachiyo, 13

the present owner's great-grandfather. Not only does it turn on the lights, but it allows you to open and close the curtains by remote control. Those on a budget might consider a room in the newer annex. Breakfast and dinner are included in the rate. *Nakahakusan-chō, Fuyachō-Anekōji-agaru, Nakagyō-ku, Kyōto-shi 604-8094, tel. 075/221–1136, fax 075/221–1139, www.hiiragiya.co.jp. 33 Japanese-style rooms, 28 with bath. AE, DC, MC, V.*

$$$$ TAWARAYA. The most famous of Kyōto's inns, this is the abode of kings and queens, princes and princesses, and presidents and dictators when they visit Kyōto. Tawaraya was founded more than 300 years ago and is currently run by the 11th generation of the Okazaki family. For all its subdued beauty and sense of tradition, the inn does have modern comforts such as heat and air-conditioning, but they hardly detract from the atmosphere of yesteryear. The rooms' superb antiques come from the Okazaki family collection. The service and food here might be disappointing, however, if you have not been recommended to the ryokan by a respected Japanese. You are given the option of staying on a European Plan basis and, if you wish, of ordering a selection of dinners from ¥12,000 to ¥60,000, the former option being rather meager. *Fuyachō-Aneyakōji-agaru, Nakagyō-ku, Kyōto-shi 604-8094, tel. 075/211–5566, fax 075/211–2204. 18 Japanese-style rooms. AE, DC, V.*

$$$–$$$$ KYŌTO BRIGHTON HOTEL. ★ The Brighton is unquestionably the city's best hotel in this price range. Its simple, clean design gives it an airy and spacious quality lacking in most other Kyōto hotels. Hallways circle a central atrium, and plants hang from the banisters of every floor. Glass elevators carry you up into the atrium to your room. Large by Japanese standards, rooms have separate seating areas with a couch and TV. No need to worry about city noise: the Brighton is on a quiet side street close to the Imperial Palace, although not within walking distance of most of Kyōto's main attractions. *Nakadachiuri, Shin-machi-dōri, Kamigyō-ku, Kyōto-shi 602-8071, tel. 075/441–4411; 800/223–6800* in the U.S.; 0800/181–123 in the U.K.; fax 075/431–2360; www.brightonhotels.co.jp. 181 rooms, 2 suites. 5 restaurants, 2 bars, pool, hair salon, shops. AE, DC, MC, V.

$$–$$$$ HOTEL GRANVIA KYŌTO. ★ Combining the traditional design elements of Kyōto in its interior with the ultramodern exterior of the Kyōto Eki building in which it is located, this hotel provides both comfort and convenience. Rooms are spacious; a standard double room has two double beds, a desk, a little sitting area, and the best combination of Western- and Japanese-style bathrooms. Sliding glass doors separate a bidet toilet and sink from the shower and bath. The showerhead is mounted on the wall next to the bathtub, allowing guests to shower outside the tub and then relax in the tub as the Japanese do. Rooms have wallpaper and decorative headboards of washi in various colors. Take some time to walk between the north and south towers along the glassed walkway, taking in the view of the city. Karasuma, Oshikoji-dori-sagaru, Kyōto-shi 600-8216, tel. 075/344–8888, fax 075/344–4400, www.granvia-kyoto.co.jp. 539 rooms. 15 restaurants, pool, hair salon, health club, shops. AE, DC, MC, V.

$$$ DAIMONJIYA. This tiny inn just off the busy shopping area of Sanjō-dōri is as famous for its guest rooms as for the food— breakfast and dinner, which are included in the room rate— served (in the guest rooms). Each room, with fine wood interiors, overlooks a small garden. Kaiseki is the specialty of the house; the chef was trained at the best Kyōto culinary establishment. You do not need to be a guest to use one of the rooms for a meal, but then you would be missing out on the quintessential ryokan experience. Nishi-Iru, Kawara-machi-Sanjō, Nakagyō-ku, Kyōto-shi 604-8031, tel. 075/221–0603. 7 Japanese-style rooms. AE, DC.

$$–$$$ ANA HOTEL KYŌTO. The best thing about this hotel is its location, directly across from Nijō-jō. If your room faces the castle rather than another high-rise, you can be assured that you are indeed in Kyōto. Now for the less-good news: off the long, narrow, rather depressing corridors are long, narrow guest rooms that could use refurbishing—especially considering the rates. There are French, Chinese, and Japanese restaurants. *Nijō-jō-mae, Horikawa-dōri, Nakagyō-ku, Kyōto-shi 604-8301, tel. 075/231-1155, fax 075/231-5333, www.anahotels.com. 303 rooms. 7 restaurants, 3 bars, indoor pool, health club, shops. AE, DC, MC, V.*

$$-$$$ HOTEL FUJITA KYŌTO. In the light of a full moon, the waterfall in
★ this pleasant hotel's garden sparkles while waterfowl play. The lobby is narrow and long, with comfortable gray armchairs playing nicely against deep red carpeting. The Fujita has Japanese and Scandinavian decor throughout, and 18 rooms have Japanese-style furnishings. The two main restaurants are a kaiseki dining room and a steak house with counter and table service. Not far from the nightlife center of Gion, this pleasant hotel is situated along the Kamo-gawa. *Nishizume, Nijō-Ōhashi, Kamo-gawa, Nakagyō-ku, Kyōto-shi 604-0902, tel. 075/222-1511, fax 075/256-4561, www.fujita-kanko.co.jp. 177 Western-style rooms, 18 Japanese-style rooms. 4 restaurants, 2 bars, hair salon, shops. AE, DC, MC, V.*

$$-$$$ KYŌTO KOKUSAI HOTEL. Across the street from Nijō-jō, Kokusai provides excellent views from the rooftop lounge and rooms on the west side of the castle and is only a few yards from the entrance to the Nijō-jō-mae stop on the Tōzai subway line. Perhaps the best reason to choose this hotel, aside from its convenient location, is the Lounge Miyabi, where you can look out through large glass windows into a beautiful courtyard garden. A stage with a thatched roof and lacquered flooring floats on the garden's pond. In the daytime, you can relax with matcha and a sweet while watching a single swan swim gracefully on the pond. At night, have your picture taken with a maiko (apprentice geisha). Then, take your seat either inside or outside to watch her perform two dances. Pictures are taken every night from 7 to 7:20, and the performance lasts from 7:20 to 7:40. Beds swathed in golden, silken duvets grace the large double rooms. Japanese-style paper screens shade the windows. *Nijō-eki-mae,*

Horikawa-dori, Nakagyō-ku, Kyōto-shi 604-8502, tel. 075/222–1111, fax 075/231–9381, www.kyoto-kokusai.com. 277 rooms. 5 restaurants, bar, 2 lounges, shops. AE, DC, MC, V.

$$–$$$ KYŌTO TŌKYŪ HOTEL. The pillared main entrance, entrance hall, and lobby are expansive, and the courtyard, with its reflecting pool and waterfall, creates a dramatic atmosphere. The well-appointed rooms of this large chain hotel, predominantly in off-white tones, are comfortable and spacious. 580 Kakimoto-chō, Gojō-sagaru, Horikawa-dōri, Shimogyō-ku, Kyōto-shi 600-8357, tel. 075/341–2411, fax 075/341–2488, www.tokyuhotel.com. 437 rooms. 3 restaurants, 2 bars, pool, hair salon, shops, travel services. AE, DC, MC, V.

$$–$$$ NEW MIYAKO HOTEL. The 10-story white edifice has two protruding wings with landscaping and street lamps reminiscent of a hotel in the United States. Its location in front of Kyōto Eki makes it attractive if you're planning train trips from the city. 17 Nishi-Kujōin-chō, Minami-ku, Kyōto-shi 601-8412, tel. 075/661–7111, fax 075/661–7135, www.mykhtls.co.jp. 71 Western-style rooms, 4 Japanese-style rooms. 3 restaurants, bar, tea shop, barbershop, shops. AE, DC, MC, V.

$$–$$$ RIHGA ROYAL HOTEL KYŌTO. The rooms at this well-established chain hotel vary in price according to size, but even the smallest rooms don't seem claustrophobic thanks to the added Japanese touch of doors made from shōji. On the 14th floor is Kyōto's only revolving restaurant, which offers splendid views of the city. There's also a branch of the Kitcho on the premises. You'll find its famous parent restaurant in western Kyōto. The hotel is only a five-minute walk from Kyōto Eki, but a shuttle bus leaves the Hachijō Guchi Exit every 15 minutes. Horikawa-Shiokōji, Shimogyō-ku, Kyōto-shi 600-8327, tel. 075/341–1121; 800/877–7107 in the U.S.; fax 075/341–3073; www.rhiga.com. 498 rooms. 6 restaurants, 3 bars, coffee shop, deli, no-smoking rooms, indoor pool, barbershop, hair salon, sauna, shops, travel services. AE, DC, MC, V.

$ HIRAIWA. Imagine the ambience of a friendly, Western-style youth hostel with tatami-mat rooms, and you have the Hiraiwa ryokan, a member of the hospitable and economical Japanese Inn Group. To be a member, inns must have English-speaking staff and provide clean, comfortable accommodations. Hiraiwa is the most popular of these inns in Kyōto; it's a great place to meet fellow travelers from around the world. Rules and regulations during your stay are posted on the walls. Guests are welcome to eat with the owners in the small kitchen. The inn has shared toilets and showers. *314 Hayao-chō, Kaminoguchi-agaru, Ninomiya-chō-dōri, Shimogyō-ku, Kyōto-shi 600-8114, tel. 075/351–6748. 21 Japanese-style rooms. AE, MC, V.*

NORTHERN KYŌTO

$$$$ TAKARAGA-IKE PRINCE HOTEL. Although some distance north of the center, Kyōto's only deluxe hotel is close to the Kokusaikaikan subway station and is especially convenient for the nearby International Conference Hall. Its unusual doughnut-shape design provides each room with a view of the surrounding mountains and forests. Inside corridors overlook an inner garden. The tasteful, spacious guest rooms are decorated with colors that complement the greenery of the outside views, and all have beds that are probably the largest you'll find in Japan. Details include impressive chandeliers all around the building, Miró prints hanging in every suite, and an authentic teahouse beside a pond. Demonstrations of the tea ceremony can be arranged upon request. The hotel offers tremendous discounts in summer; check out the Web site for special packages. *Takaraga-ike, Sakyō-ku, Kyōto-shi 606-8505, tel. 075/712–1111; 800/542–8686 in the U.S.; fax 075/712–7677; www2.princehotels.co.jp. 322 rooms. 3 restaurants, 2 bars, tea shops. AE, DC, MC, V.*

practical information

Addresses

Even Japanese people cannot find a building based on the address alone. If you get in a taxi with a written address, do not assume the driver will be able to find your destination. Usually, people provide very detailed instructions or maps to explain their exact locations. It's always good to **know the location of your destination in relation to a major building** or department store.

Air Travel

CARRIERS
➤ **AIRLINES & CONTACTS: American** (tel. 800/433–7300; 0120/000–860 in Japan). **All Nippon Airways** (tel. 800/235–9262; 020/7355–1155 in the U.K.; 03/5489–8800 in Japan for domestic flights; 0120/5489–8800 in Japan for international flights). **British Airways** (tel. 0345/222–111 in the U.K.; 03/3593–8811 in Japan). **Canadian Airlines** (tel. 888/247–2262; 03/3281–7426 in Japan). **Continental** (tel. 800/525–0280). **Delta** (tel. 800/221–1212). **Japan Air System** (tel. 03/3438–1155 in Japan for domestic flights; 0120/511–283 in Japan for international flights). **Japan Airlines** (tel. 800/525–3663; 0345/747–700 in the U.K.; 0120/25–5931 in Japan). **Korean Air** (tel. 800/438–5000; 0800/413–000 in the U.K.; 03/5443–3311 in Japan). **Lufthansa** (tel. 0345/737–747 in the U.K.). **Northwest** (tel. 800/447–4747). **Swissair** (tel. 800/221–4750; 020/7434–7300 in the U.K.; 03/3533–6000 or 0120/120–747 in Japan). **Thai Airways International** (tel. 800/426–5204; 020/7499–9113 in the

U.K.; 03/3503–3311 in Japan). **United** (tel. 800/241–6522; 0120/114–466 in Japan).

FLYING TIMES

Flying time to Japan is 13¾ hours from New York, 12¾ hours from Chicago, 9¼ hours from Los Angeles, and 11–12 hours from the United Kingdom.

Airports & Airport Transfers

The closest international airport to Kyōto is Kansai International Airport (KIX), near Ōsaka. KIX does have domestic flights, particularly to major cities, but the majority of internal air traffic uses Ōsaka's Itami Airport. The major gateway to Japan is Tōkyō's Narita Airport (NRT). Flight time between Tōkyō and Ōsaka is about 70 minutes.

AIRPORT TRANSFERS

From KIX to Kyōto Eki, take the JR Haruka Limited Express, which departs every 30 minutes to make the 75-minute run and costs ¥3,490 including charges for a reserved seat; or use a JR Pass. From Itami, buses depart for Kyōto approximately every 20 minutes from 8:10 AM to 9:20 PM. Some stop at major hotels, but most go straight to Kyōto Eki. The trip takes from 55 to 90 minutes and costs ¥1,280 or ¥1,370, depending on the Kyōto destination.

Taxis cost more than ¥10,000 from KIX and Itami to Kyōto.

➤ **AIRPORT INFORMATION: Itami Airport** (tel. 06/6856–6781). **Kansai International Airport** (tel. 0724/55–2500). **Narita Airport** (tel. 0476/34–5000).

Bus Travel

TO AND FROM KYŌTO

Japan Railways offers a number of overnight long-distance buses that are not very comfortable but are inexpensive. You can use Japan Rail Passes (☞ Train Travel) on these buses.

➤ **BUS INFORMATION: Japan Railways** (tel. 03/3423–0111), open weekdays 10–6.

WITHIN KYŌTO

A network of bus routes covers the entire city. Most city buses run 7 AM–9 PM daily, but a few start as early as 5:30 AM and run until 11 PM. The main bus terminals are Kyōto Eki, Keihan Sanjō Eki, Karasuma-Kitao-ji, and at the Shijō-dōri–Karasuma-dōri intersection. Many city buses do not have signs in English, so you'll need to **know the bus number.** You should **pick up a bus map** early in your stay from the Tourist Information Center at the Kyōto Tower Building, across from JR Kyōto Eki.

At each bus stop a guidepost indicates the stop name, the bus route, and the bus-route number. Because the information at most guideposts is only in Japanese (except for the route number, which is given as an Arabic numeral), you are advised to **ask your hotel clerk beforehand to write down your destination in Japanese, along with the route number,** to show to the bus driver and fellow passengers; this will allow the driver and others to help you if you get lost. You might also ask your hotel clerk beforehand how many stops your ride will take.

Within the city the standard fare is ¥220, which you pay before leaving the bus; outside the city limits the fare varies according to distance. Several special transportation passes are available, including the following: a one-day city bus pass for ¥500; a multiday discount bus pass that provides ¥2,250 worth of riding for ¥2,000; and the *torafikka kyō* pass, which provides ¥3,300 worth of transport via city bus or subway for ¥3,000. Additionally, you can purchase combination one-day (¥1,200) or two-day (¥2,000) passes that cover travel on city buses, the subway, and private Kyōto Line buses, with restrictions on some routes. The ¥3,000 *surutto Kansai*, a versatile multiday pass, covers transportation on city buses, the subway, and all the major Kansai railways except the JR line. All of these passes are sold at travel agencies, main bus terminals, and information centers in Kyōto Eki.

You can use a JR Pass on the local bus that travels between Kyōto Eki and Takao (in northwestern Kyōto), passing close to Nijō Eki.

Car Rental

Rates in Kyōto begin at $87 a day and $437 a week for an economy car with unlimited mileage. This does not include tax, which is 5% on car rentals. Reservations in the United States should be made at least a week in advance.

➤ **MAJOR AGENCIES: Avis** (tel. 800/331–1084; 800/879–2847 in Canada; 02/9353–9000 in Australia; 09/525–1982 in New Zealand; 0870/606–0100 in the U.K., www.avis.com). **Budget** (tel. 800/527–0700; 0870/156–5656 in the U.K., www.budget.com). **Dollar** (tel. 800/800–6000, 0124/622–0111 in the U.K., where it's affiliated with Sixt; 02/9223–1444 in Australia, www.dollar.com). **Hertz** (tel. 800/654–3001; 800/263–0600 in Canada; 020/8897–2072 in the U.K.; 02/9669–2444 in Australia; 09/256–8690 in New Zealand, www.hertz.com) **National Car Rental** (tel. 800/227–7368; 020/8680–4800 in the U.K., www.nationalcar.com).

INSURANCE

When driving a rented car you are generally responsible for any damage to or loss of the vehicle as well as for any property damage or personal injury that you may cause. Before you rent, see what coverage your personal auto-insurance policy and credit cards provide.

REQUIREMENTS & RESTRICTIONS

In Japan your own driver's license is not acceptable. You need an international driver's permit; it's available from the American or Canadian Automobile Association, or, in the United Kingdom, from the Automobile Association or Royal Automobile Club.

SURCHARGES

Before you pick up a car in one city and leave it in another, ask about drop-off charges or one-way service fees, which can be substantial. Note, too, that some rental agencies charge extra if you return the car before the time specified in your contract. To avoid a hefty refueling fee, fill the tank just before you turn in the car, but be aware that gas stations near the rental outlet may overcharge.

Car Travel

Car travel along the Tōkyō–Kyōto–Hiroshima corridor is not as convenient as the trains. Within Kyōto buses and subways often get you to your destinations faster and more comfortably. Roads are congested, gas is expensive (about ¥100 per liter, or $4.80 per gallon), and highway tolls are exorbitant. Within Kyōto English signs are few and far between, one-way streets often lead you off the track, and parking is often hard to find and usually expensive.

Having said that, it is possible for foreigners to drive in Japan with an international driver's license (to obtain a license, contact your country's major auto club). Major roads are sufficiently marked in the roman alphabet. However, it's a good idea to have a detailed map with names written in *kanji* (Japanese characters) and *romaji* (romanized Japanese).

ROAD CONDITIONS

Roads in Japan are often narrower than those found in the United States, but they're well maintained in general.

RULES OF THE ROAD

In Japan people drive on the left. Speed limits vary, but generally the limit is 80 kph (50 mph) on highways, 40 kph (25 mph) in cities.

Consulates

The nearest consulates are in Ōsaka.

➤ **CONSULATES: Canada** (2–2–3 Nishi-Shin-Sai-bashi, Chūō-ku, Ōsaka, tel. 06/6212–4910). **U.K.** (Seiko Ōsaka Bldg., 19th floor, 35–1 Bakuro-machi, Chūō-ku, Ōsaka, tel. 06/6281–1616). **U.S.** (2–11–5 Nishi-Tenma, Kita-ku, Ōsaka, tel. 06/6315–5900).

Customs & Duties

When shopping, keep receipts for all purchases. Upon reentering the country, be ready to show customs officials what you've bought. If you feel a duty is incorrect or object to the way your clearance was handled, note the inspector's badge number and ask to see a supervisor. If the problem isn't resolved, write to the appropriate authorities, beginning with the port director at your point of entry.

IN AUSTRALIA
Australian residents who are 18 or older may bring home $A400 worth of souvenirs and gifts (including jewelry), 250 cigarettes or 250 grams of tobacco, and 1,125 ml of alcohol (including wine, beer, and spirits). Residents under 18 may bring back $A200 worth of goods. Prohibited items include meat products. Seeds, plants, and fruits need to be declared upon arrival.

➤ **INFORMATION: Australian Customs Service** (Regional Director, Box 8, Sydney, NSW 2001, Australia, tel. 02/9213–2000, fax 02/9213–4000, www.customs.gov.au).

IN CANADA
Canadian residents who have been out of Canada for at least seven days may bring home C$750 worth of goods duty-free. If you've been away fewer than seven days but more than 48 hours, the duty-free allowance drops to C$200; if your trip lasts 24–48 hours, the allowance is C$50. You may not pool

allowances with family members. Goods claimed under the C$750 exemption may follow you by mail; those claimed under the lesser exemptions must accompany you. Alcohol and tobacco products may be included in the seven-day and 48-hour exemptions but not in the 24-hour exemption. If you meet the age requirements of the province or territory through which you reenter Canada, you may bring in, duty-free, 1.14 liters (40 imperial ounces) of wine or liquor or 24 12-ounce cans or bottles of beer or ale. If you are 19 or older you may bring in, duty-free, 200 cigarettes and 50 cigars. Check ahead of time with the Canada Customs Revenue Agency or the Department of Agriculture for policies regarding meat products, seeds, plants, and fruits.

You may send an unlimited number of gifts worth up to C$60 each duty-free to Canada. Label the package UNSOLICITED GIFT—VALUE UNDER $60. Alcohol and tobacco are excluded.

➤ **INFORMATION: Canada Customs Revenue Agency** (2265 St. Laurent Blvd. S, Ottawa, Ontario K1G 4K3, Canada, tel. 204/983–3500 or 506/636–5064; 800/461–9999 in Canada, www.ccra-adrc.gc.ca).

IN JAPAN
Japan has strict regulations about bringing firearms, pornography, and narcotics into the country. Anyone caught with drugs is liable to be detained, deported, and refused reentry into Japan. Certain fresh fruits, vegetables, plants, and animals are also illegal. Nonresidents are allowed to bring in duty-free: (1) 400 cigarettes or 100 cigars or 500 grams of tobacco; (2) three bottles of alcohol; (3) 2 ounces of perfume; (4) other goods up to ¥200,000 value.

IN NEW ZEALAND
Homeward-bound residents 17 or older may bring back $700 worth of souvenirs and gifts. Your duty-free allowance also

includes 4.5 liters of wine or beer; one 1,125-ml bottle of spirits; and either 200 cigarettes, 250 grams of tobacco, 50 cigars, or a combination of the three up to 250 grams. Prohibited items include meat products, seeds, plants, and fruits.

➤ **INFORMATION: New Zealand Customs** (Custom House, 50 Anzac Ave., Box 29, Auckland, New Zealand, tel. 09/300–5399, fax 09/359–6730, www.customs.govt.nz).

IN THE U.K.
From countries outside the European Union, including Japan, you may bring home, duty-free, 200 cigarettes or 50 cigars; 1 liter of spirits or 2 liters of fortified or sparkling wine or liqueurs; 2 liters of still table wine; 60 ml of perfume; 250 ml of toilet water; plus £145 worth of other goods, including gifts and souvenirs. If returning from outside the EU, prohibited items include meat products, seeds, plants, and fruits.

➤ **INFORMATION: HM Customs and Excise** (St. Christopher House, Southwark, London SE1 OTE, U.K., tel. 020/7928–3344, www.hmce.gov.uk).

IN THE U.S.
U.S. residents who have been out of the country for at least 48 hours (and who have not used the $400 allowance or any part of it in the past 30 days) may bring home $400 worth of foreign goods duty-free.

U.S. residents 21 and older may bring back 1 liter of alcohol duty-free. In addition, regardless of your age, you are allowed 200 cigarettes and 100 non-Cuban cigars. Antiques, which the U.S. Customs Service defines as objects more than 100 years old, enter duty-free, as do original works of art done entirely by hand, including paintings, drawings, and sculptures.

You may also mail or ship packages home duty-free: up to $200 worth of goods for personal use, with a limit of one parcel per addressee per day (except alcohol or tobacco products or perfume worth more than $5); label the package PERSONAL USE and attach a list of its contents and their retail value. Do not label the package UNSOLICITED GIFT or your duty-free exemption will drop to $100. Mailed items do not affect your duty-free allowance on your return.

➤ **INFORMATION: U.S. Customs Service** (1300 Pennsylvania Ave. NW, Room 6.3D, Washington, DC 20229, www.customs.gov; inquiries tel. 202/354–1000; complaints c/o 1300 Pennsylvania Ave. NW, Room 5.4D, Washington, DC 20229; registration of equipment c/o Office of Passenger Programs, tel. 202/927–0530).

Dining

Food, like many other things in Kyōto, is expensive. Eating at hotels and famous restaurants is costly; however, you can eat well and reasonably at standard restaurants that may not have signs in English. Many less expensive restaurants have plastic replicas of the dishes they serve displayed in their front windows, so you can always point to what you want to eat if the language barrier is insurmountable. A good place to look for moderately priced dining spots is in the restaurant concourse of department stores, usually on the bottom floor.

In general, Kyōto restaurants are very clean. The water is safe, even when drawn from a tap.

Unless otherwise noted, the restaurants listed in this guide are open daily for lunch and dinner.

Electricity

To use electric-powered equipment purchased in the United States or Canada, **bring a converter and adapter.** The electrical current in Kyōto is 100 volts, 60 cycles alternating current (AC); the United States runs on 110-volt, 60-cycle AC current. Wall outlets in Kyōto accept plugs with two flat prongs, like in the United States, but do not accept U.S. three-prong plugs.

If your appliances are dual-voltage, you'll need only an adapter. Don't use 110-volt outlets marked FOR SHAVERS ONLY for high-wattage appliances such as blow-dryers. Most laptops operate equally well on 110 and 220 volts and so require only an adapter.

Emergencies

The Sakabe Clinic has 24-hour emergency facilities.

Assistance in English is available 24 hours a day on the toll-free Japan Helpline.

➤ **DOCTORS: Daiichi Sekijuji** (Red Cross Hospital; Higashiyama Hon-machi, Higashiyama-ku, tel. 075/561–1121). **Daini Sekijuji Byoin** (Second Red Cross Hospital; Kamanza-dōri, Maruta-machi-agaru, Kamigyō-ku, tel. 075/231–5171). **Japan Baptist Hospital** (Kita-Shirakawa, Yamanomoto-chō, Sakyō-ku, tel. 075/781–5191). **Sakabe Clinic** (435 Yamamoto-chō, Gokō-machi, Nijō Sagaru, Nakagyō-ku, tel. 075/231–1624).

➤ **EMERGENCY SERVICES: Ambulance** (tel. 119). **Japan Helpline** (tel. 0120/461–997). **Police** (tel. 110).

English-Language Media

BOOKS
➤ **BOOKSTORES: Izumiya Book Center** (Avanti Bldg. across from Kyōto Eki, on Shinkansen side, 6th floor, Minami-ku, tel. 075/671–8987). **Maruzen Kyōto** (296 Kawara-machi-dōri, Nakagyō-ku, tel. 075/241–2169). **Media Shop** (Vox Bldg., 1st floor, Kawara-machi, San-jō, Nakagyō-ku, tel. 075/255–0783).

NEWSPAPERS AND MAGAZINES
The monthly *Kansai Time Out* publishes comprehensive events listings for Kyōto. It costs ¥300 and is available in major hotels

and bookshops. The *Daily Yomiuri*, the *Japan Times*, and the *International Herald Tribune* are reliable for national and international news coverage in English, as well as for entertainment reviews and listings. They're available at newsstands and in bookstores that carry English-language books.

Etiquette & Behavior

It is customary to **bow upon meeting someone.** The art of bowing is not simple; the depth of your bow depends on your social position in respect to that of the other person. Younger people, or those of lesser status, must bow deeper in order to indicate their respect and acknowledge their position. You're not expected to understand the complexity of these rules, and a basic nod of the head will suffice. Many Japanese are familiar with Western customs and will offer a hand for a handshake.

Most entertaining among Japanese is done in restaurants or bars. It's an honor when you are invited to a home. If you do receive an invitation, bring along a small gift—a souvenir from your country makes the best present, but food and liquor or anything that can be consumed (and not take up space in the home) is also appreciated. Upon entering a home, **remove your shoes in the foyer and put on the slippers that are provided;** in Japan shoes are for wearing outdoors only. Be sure your socks or stockings are in good condition.

Japanese restaurants often provide a small hot towel called an *oshibori*. This is to wipe your hands but not your face. When you are finished with your oshibori, fold or roll it up. If you're not accustomed to eating with chopsticks, ask for a fork instead. When taking food from a shared dish, do not use the part of the chopsticks that has entered your mouth to pick up a morsel. Instead, use the end that you have been holding in your hand. Never leave your chopsticks sticking upright in your food; this is how rice offerings at funerals are arranged. Instead, rest chopsticks on the edge of the tray, bowl, or plate between bites and at the end of the meal.

BUSINESS ETIQUETTE

In Japan, *meishi* (business cards) are mandatory. Upon meeting someone for the first time, it is common to bow and to proffer your business card simultaneously. Although English will suffice on your business card, it's best to have one side printed in Japanese (there are outfits in Japan that provide this service in 24 hours). In a sense, the cards are simply a convenience. Japanese sometimes have difficulty with Western names, and referring to the cards is helpful. Also, in a society where hierarchy matters, Japanese like to know job titles and rank, so it's useful if your card indicates your position in your company. Japanese often place the business cards they have received in front of them on a table or desk as they conduct their meetings. Follow suit.

Be prompt for both social and business occasions. Japanese addresses tend to be complicated, and traffic is often heavy, so allow for adequate travel time. Most Japanese are not accustomed to using first names in business circumstances. Unless you are sure that the Japanese person is extremely comfortable with Western customs, it is best to **stick to last names and use the honorific word** *-san* **after the name,** as in *Tanaka-san* (Mr. or Mrs. Tanaka). Also, respect the hierarchy, and as much as possible address yourself to the most senior person in the room.

Don't be frustrated if decisions are not made instantly. Rarely empowered to make decisions, individual businesspeople must confer with their colleagues and superiors. Even if you are annoyed, **don't express anger or aggression.** Losing one's temper is equated with losing face in Japan.

A separation of business and private lives remains sacrosanct in Japan, and it is best not to ask about personal matters. Rather than asking about a person's family, it is better to **stick to neutral subjects in conversation.**

Usually, entertaining is done over dinner, followed by an evening on the town. Drinking is something of a national pastime in Japan. If you would rather not suffer from a hangover the next day, do not refuse your drink—sip, but keep your glass at least half full. Because the custom is for companions to pour drinks for each other, an empty glass is nearly the equivalent of requesting another drink. **Don't pour your own drink, and if a glass at your table happens to be empty, show your attentiveness by filling it for your companion.**

A special note to women traveling on business in Japan: remember that although the situation is gradually changing, many Japanese women do not have careers. Many Japanese businessmen do not yet know how to interact with Western businesswomen. They may be uncomfortable, aloof, or patronizing. Be patient and, if the need arises, gently remind them that, professionally, you expect to be treated as any man would be.

Health

Tap water everywhere is safe in Kyōto. It may be difficult to buy the standard over-the-counter remedies you're used to, so it's best to bring with you any medications (in their proper packaging) you may need.

Holidays

Peak times for travel in Japan tend to fall around holiday periods. You'll want to avoid traveling during the few days before and after New Year's; during Golden Week, which follows

Greenery Day (April 29); and in mid-July and mid-August, at the time of Obon festivals, when many Japanese return to their hometowns (Obon festivals are celebrated July or August 13–16, depending on the location). When a holiday falls on a Sunday, the following Monday is a holiday.

January 1 (*Ganjitsu*, New Year's Day); the second Monday in January (*Senjin-no-hi*, Coming of Age Day); February 11 (*Kenkoku Kinen-no-bi*, National Foundation Day); March 20 or 21 (*Shumbun-no-hi*, Vernal Equinox); April 29 (*Midori-no-hi*, Greenery Day); May 3 (*Kempo Kinen-bi*, Constitution Day); May 5 (*Kodomo-no-hi*, Children's Day); September 15 (*Keiro-no-hi*, Respect for the Aged Day); September 23 or 24 (*Shubun-no-hi*, Autumnal Equinox); the second Monday in October (*Taiiku-no-hi*, Sports Day); November 3 (*Bunka-no-hi*, Culture Day); November 23 (*Kinro Kansha-no-hi*, Labor Thanksgiving Day); December 23 (*Tennō Tanjobi*, Emperor's Birthday).

Language

Communicating in Japan can be a challenge. This is not because the Japanese don't speak English but because most of us know little, if any, Japanese. Take some time before you leave home to **learn a few basic words**, such as where (*doko*), what time (*nan-ji*), bathroom (*o-te-arai*), thank you (*arigatō gozaimasu*), excuse me (*sumimasen*), and please (*onegai shimasu*).

Most Japanese study English in school for nearly a decade. This does not mean everyone *speaks* English. Schools emphasize reading, writing, and grammar. As a result, many Japanese can read English but can speak only a few basic phrases. Furthermore, when asked, "Do you speak English?" many Japanese, out of modesty, say no, even if they do understand and speak a fair amount of it. It is usually best to simply ask what you really want to know slowly, clearly, and as simply as possible.

Although a local may understand your simple question, he or she cannot always give you an answer that requires complicated instructions. Be sure to **ask more than one person for directions every step of the way.** Also, remember that politeness is a matter of course in Japan and that the Japanese won't want to lose face by saying that they don't know how to get somewhere. If the situation gets confusing, **bow, say** *arigatō gozaimashita* **("thank you" in the past tense), and ask someone else.** Even though you are communicating on a very basic level, misunderstandings can happen easily.

Traveling in parts of Kyōto can be problematic if you don't read Japanese. Before you leave home, **buy a phrase book** that shows English, English transliterations of Japanese (*romaji*), and Japanese characters (*kanji* and *kana*). You can read the romaji to pick up a few Japanese words and match the kanji and kana in the phrase book with characters on signs and menus. When all else fails, ask for help by pointing to the Japanese words in your book.

Learning Japanese is a major commitment. Japanese writing alone consists of three character systems: kanji, characters borrowed and adapted from China centuries ago, which represent ideas; and two forms of kana—*hiragana* and *katakana*—which represent sounds. Hiragana is used to write some Japanese words, verb inflections, and adjectives; katakana is used for foreign words, slang expressions, and technical terms. There are two sets of 47 kana and more than 6,000 kanji, although most Japanese use fewer than 1,000 kanji.

The most common system of writing Japanese words in Roman letters is the modified Hepburn system, which spells out Japanese words phonetically and is followed in this book.

For information on pronouncing Japanese words, notes on how Japanese words are rendered in this guide, and a list of useful words and phrases, *see* An English-Japanese Traveler's Vocabulary.

Lodging

Overnight accommodations in Kyōto run from luxury hotels to *ryokan* (traditional inns) to youth hostels.

The lodgings we list are the cream of the crop in each price category. We always list the facilities that are available—but we don't specify whether they cost extra: when pricing accommodations, always ask what's included and what costs extra.

HOME VISITS

You can get a sense of domestic life in Japan by visiting a local family in their home. The program is voluntary on the home owner's part, and there is no charge for a visit. To make a reservation, apply in writing for a home visit at least a day in advance to the local tourist information office of the place you are visiting. Contact the Japan National Tourist Organization (☞ Visitor Information) before leaving for Japan for more information on the program.

HOTELS

Full-service, first-class hotels in Kyōto resemble their counterparts all over the world, and because many of the staff members speak English, these are the easiest places for foreigners to stay. They are also among the most expensive.

Business hotels are a reasonable alternative. They are clean, impersonal, and functional. All have Western-style rooms that vary from small to minuscule; service is minimal. However, every room has a private bathroom, albeit cramped, with tub and handheld shower, television (with Japanese-language channels), telephone, and a hot-water thermos. Business hotels are often conveniently located near the railway station. The staff may not speak English, and there is usually no room service.

INEXPENSIVE ACCOMMODATIONS

JNTO publishes a listing of some 200 accommodations that welcome foreigners and are reasonably priced. To be listed, properties must meet Japanese fire codes and charge less than ¥8,000 per person without meals. Properties include business hotels, (☞ ryokan) of a very rudimentary nature, (☞ minshuku), and pensions. It's the luck of the draw whether you choose a good or less-than-good property. In most cases rooms are clean but very small. Except in business hotels, shared baths are the norm, and you are expected to have your room lights out by 10 PM.

Many establishments on the list of reasonably priced accommodations can be reserved through the nonprofit organization **Welcome Inn Reservation Center.** Reservation forms are available from your nearest JNTO office (☞ Visitor Information). The Japanese Inn Group, which provides reasonable accommodations for foreign visitors, can be reserved through this same service. The center must receive reservation requests at least one week before your departure. If you are already in Japan, JNTO's Tourist Information Center can make immediate reservations for you at these Welcome Inns.

➤ **RESERVATIONS: Welcome Inn Reservation Center** (Tōkyō International Forum B1, 3–5–1 Marunouchi, Chiyoda-ku, Tōkyō 100–0005, tel. 03/3211–4201, fax 03/3211–9009).

MINSHUKU

Minshuku are private homes that accept guests. Usually they cost about ¥6,000 per person, including two meals. Don't be surprised if you are expected to lay out and put away your own bedding in a minshuku. Meals are often served in communal dining rooms. Minshuku vary in size and atmosphere; some are private homes that take in only a few guests, while others are more like no-frill inns. Some of your most memorable stays could be at a minshuku, as they offer a chance to become acquainted with a Japanese family and their hospitality.

➤ **INFORMATION: Japan Minshuku Center** (Tōkyō Kōtsū, Kaikan Building, B1, 2–10–1 Yūrakuchō, Chiyoda-ku, Tōkyō, tel. 03/3216–6556, fax 03/3216–6557, www.minshuku.co.jp).

RYOKAN

If you want to sample the Japanese way, **spend at least one night in a ryokan (inn).** Usually small, one- or two-story wooden structures with a garden or scenic view, they provide traditional Japanese accommodations: simple rooms in which the bedding is rolled out onto the floor at night.

Ryokan vary in price and quality. Some older, long-established inns cost as much as ¥80,000 per person, whereas humbler places that are more like bed-and-breakfasts are as low as ¥6,000. Prices are per person and include the cost of breakfast, dinner, and tax. Some inns allow you to stay without having dinner and lower the cost accordingly. However, this is not recommended, because the service and meals are part of the ryokan experience.

It is important to **follow Japanese customs in all ryokan.** Upon entering, **take off your shoes** and put on the slippers that are provided in the entryway. A maid, after bowing to welcome you, will escort you to your room, which will have tatami (straw mats) on the floor and will probably be partitioned off with shōji (sliding paper-paneled walls). Remove your slippers before entering your room; you should not step on the tatami with either shoes or slippers. The room will have little furniture or decoration—perhaps one small low table and cushions on the tatami, with a long, simple scroll on the wall. Often the rooms overlook a garden.

Plan to arrive in the late afternoon, as is the custom. After relaxing with a cup of green tea, have a long, hot bath. In ryokan with thermal pools, you can take to the waters anytime, although the doors to the pool are usually locked from 11 PM to 6 AM. In ryokan without thermal baths or private baths in guest rooms, guests must stagger visits to the one or two public baths. Typically the maid will ask what time you would like your bath and fit you into a schedule. In Japanese baths, washing and soaking are separate functions: wash and rinse off entirely, and then get in the tub. Be sure to keep all soap out of the tub. Because other guests will be using the same bathwater after you, it is important to observe this custom. After your bath, change into a *yukata*, a simple cotton kimono, provided in your room. Don't worry about walking around in what is essentially a robe—all other guests will be doing the same.

Dinner, included in the price, is served in your room at smaller and more personal ryokan; at larger ryokan, meals may be in the dining room. After you are finished, a maid will discreetly come in, clear away the dishes, and lay out your futon. In Japan *futon* means bedding, and this consists of a thin cotton mattress and a comforter. The small, hard pillow is filled with grain. In the morning a maid will gently wake you, clear away the futon, and bring in your Japanese-style breakfast, which often consists of fish, pickled vegetables, and rice.

Because most ryokan staffs are small and dedicated, it is important to be considerate and understanding of their somewhat rigid schedules. Guests are expected to arrive in the late afternoon and eat around 6. Usually the doors to the inn are locked at 10, so plan for early evenings. Breakfast is served around 8, and checkout is at 10.

A genuine traditional ryokan with exemplary service is exorbitantly expensive—more than ¥30,000–¥90,000 per person per night with two meals. Many modern hotels with

Japanese-style rooms are now referring to themselves as ryokan, and though meals may be served in the guests' rooms, they are a far cry from the traditional ryokan. There are also small inns claiming the status of ryokan, but they are really nothing more than bed-and-breakfast establishments where meals are taken in a communal dining room—for an additional fee—and service is minimal. In lesser-priced inns, which run from ¥6,000 for a single room to ¥7,000 for a double, tubs are likely to be plastic rather than cedarwood, and small rooms might overlook a street rather than a garden. Rooms have tatami straw mat floors, futon bedding, and a scroll and/or flower arrangement in its rightful place. JNTO offers a publication listing some of these.

Not all inns are willing to accept foreign guests because of language and cultural barriers. This makes calling ahead for a room important so you can be sure to get one. Top-level ryokan expect even new Japanese guests to have introductions and references from a respected client of the inn, which means that you, too, might need an introduction from a Japanese. On the other side of this issue, inns that do accept foreigners without introduction sometimes treat them as cash cows, which means giving you cursory service and a lesser room. When you reserve a room, try to have a Japanese make the call for you, or you can do it yourself if you know Japanese; this will convey the idea that you understand the customs of staying in a traditional inn.

➤ **INFORMATION: Japan Ryokan Association** (1–8–3 Maru-no-uchi, Chiyoda-ku, Tōkyō, tel. 03/3231–5310). **JNTO** (☞ Visitor Information).

TEMPLES

You can arrange accommodations in Buddhist temples. JNTO has lists of temples that accept guests. A stay at a temple generally costs ¥3,000–¥9,000 per night, including two meals. Some temples offer instruction in meditation or allow you to observe their religious practices, while others simply offer a room. The Japanese-style rooms are very simple and range from beautiful, quiet havens to not-so-comfortable, basic cubicles.

Mail & Shipping

The Japanese postal service is very efficient. Air mail between Japan and the United States takes between five and eight days. Surface mail can take anywhere from four to eight weeks. Express service is also available through post offices.

Money Matters

Kyōto is expensive, but there are ways to cut costs. One good way to hold down expenses is to **avoid taxis** (they tend to get stuck in traffic anyway) and **try the inexpensive, efficient bus systems.** Instead of going to a restaurant with menus in English and Western-style food, go to places where you can rely on your good old index finger to point to the dish you want, and **try food that the Japanese eat.**

A cup of coffee costs ¥350–¥600; a bottle of beer, ¥350–¥1,000; a McDonald's hamburger, ¥340; a bowl of noodles, ¥700.

Prices throughout this guide are given for adults. Substantially reduced fees are almost always available for children, students, and senior citizens.

CREDIT CARDS

MasterCard and Visa are the most widely accepted credit cards in Kyōto. Throughout this guide, the following abbreviations are used: **AE,** American Express; **DC,** Diners Club; **MC,** MasterCard; and **V,** Visa.

➤ **REPORTING LOST CARDS: American Express** (tel. 03/3220–6100). **Diners Club** (tel. 03/3499–1181). **MasterCard** (tel. 0031/113–886). **Visa** (tel. 0120/133–173).

CURRENCY

The unit of currency in Japan is the yen (¥). There are bills of ¥10,000, ¥5,000, ¥2,000, and ¥1,000. Coins are ¥500, ¥100, ¥50, ¥10, ¥5, and ¥1. Japanese currency floats on the international monetary exchange, so changes can be dramatic. Some vending machines will not accept the newly introduced ¥2,000 bill or the new version of the ¥500 coin, but these older machines are gradually being replaced. At press time the exchange rate was about ¥128 to the U.S. dollar, ¥81 to the Canadian dollar, and ¥186 to the pound sterling.

CURRENCY EXCHANGE

For the most favorable rates, **change money through banks.** Although ATM transaction fees may be higher abroad than at home, ATM rates are excellent because they are based on wholesale rates offered only by major banks. You won't do as well at exchange booths in airports or rail and bus stations, in hotels, in restaurants, or in stores. To avoid lines at airport exchange booths, **get a bit of local currency before you leave home.**

➤ **EXCHANGE SERVICES: International Currency Express** (tel. 888/278–6628 for orders, www.foreignmoney.com). **Thomas Cook Currency Services** (tel. 800/287–7362 for telephone orders and retail locations, www.us.thomascook.com).

Packing

Because porters can be hard to find and baggage restrictions on international flights are tight, **pack light.** Pack as you would for any American or European city. At more expensive restaurants and nightclubs, men usually need to wear a jacket and tie, and women need a dress or skirt. Wear conservative-color clothing at business meetings. Casual clothes are fine for sightseeing. Jeans are perfectly acceptable for informal dining and sightseeing.

Although there are no strict dress codes for visiting temples and shrines, you will be out of place in shorts or immodest outfits. You'll need sturdy walking shoes for the gravel pathways that surround temples and fill parks. Make sure to bring comfortable clothing that isn't too tight to wear in traditional Japanese restaurants, where you may need to sit on tatami-matted floors.

Japanese do not wear shoes in private homes or in any temples or traditional inns. Having shoes you can quickly slip in and out of is a decided advantage.

If you're a morning coffee addict, **take along packets of instant coffee.** All lodgings provide a thermos of hot water and bags of green tea in every room, but for coffee you'll either have to call room service (which can be expensive) or buy very sweet coffee in a can from a vending machine. If you're staying in a Japanese inn, it probably won't have coffee, and it may be hard to find in rural areas.

Take along small gift items, such as scarves or perfume sachets, to thank hosts (on both business and pleasure trips), whether you've been invited to their home or out to a restaurant.

In your carry-on luggage, **pack an extra pair of eyeglasses or contact lenses and enough of any medication** you take to last the entire trip. You may also ask your doctor to write a spare prescription using the drug's generic name, since brand names may vary from country to country. In luggage to be checked, **never pack prescription drugs or valuables.** To avoid customs delays, carry medications in their original packaging. And don't forget to carry with you the addresses of offices that handle refunds of lost traveler's checks.

Passports & Visas

When traveling internationally, **carry your passport** even if you don't need one (it's always the best form of I.D.) and **make two**

photocopies of the data page (one for someone at home and another for you, carried separately from your passport). If you lose your passport, promptly call the nearest embassy or consulate and the local police.

ENTERING JAPAN

Visitors from the United States, Canada, Great Britain, Australia, and New Zealand can enter Japan for up to 90 days with a valid passport; no visa is required.

PASSPORT OFFICES

The best time to apply for a passport or to renew is in fall and winter. Before any trip, check your passport's expiration date, and, if necessary, renew it as soon as possible.

➤ **AUSTRALIAN CITIZENS: Australian Passport Office** (tel. 131–232, www.dfat.gov.au/passports).

➤ **CANADIAN CITIZENS: Passport Office** (tel. 819/994–3500; 800/567–6868 in Canada, www.dfait-maeci.gc.ca/passport).

➤ **NEW ZEALAND CITIZENS: New Zealand Passport Office** (tel. 04/494–0700, www.passports.govt.nz).

➤ **U.K. CITIZENS: London Passport Office** (tel. 0870/521–0410, www.ukpa.gov.uk) for fees and documentation requirements and to request an emergency passport.

➤ **U.S. CITIZENS: National Passport Information Center** (tel. 900/225–5674; calls are 35¢ per minute for automated service, $1.05 per minute for operator service, www.travel.state.gov/npicinfo.html).

Rest Rooms

The most hygienic rest rooms are in hotels and department stores and are usually clearly marked with international symbols. You may encounter Japanese-style toilets, with bowls recessed into the floor, over which you squat facing the hood.

In many homes and Japanese-style public places, there will be a pair of slippers at the entrance to the rest rooms. Change into these before entering the room, and change back when you exit.

Sightseeing Tours

EXCURSIONS

Hozugawa Yūsen organizes excursions down a 15-km (9-mi) stretch (about 90 minutes) of the Hozu Rapids in flat-bottom boats, from Kameoka to Arashiyama, which cost ¥3,900. Sunrise Tours, a subsidiary of Japan Travel Bureau, conducts full- and half-day tours to Nara and Ōsaka. An afternoon tour to Nara costs ¥6,300. Morning and afternoon trips to Ōsaka, for ¥8,900 and ¥6,200, respectively, are not worth the cost, especially if you have a JR Pass.

➤ TOUR INFORMATION: Hozugawa Yūsen (tel. 0771/225–846). Sunrise Tours (tel. 075/341–1413).

ORIENTATION TOURS

Sunrise Tours organizes half-day morning and afternoon coach tours highlighting different city attractions. Pickup service is provided from major hotels. A ¥5,300 morning tour commonly covers Nijō-jō, Kinkaku-ji, Kyōto Imperial Palace, Higashi-Hongan-ji, and the Kyōto Handicraft Center. A ¥5,300 afternoon tour includes the Heian Jingū, Sanjūsangen-dō, and Kiyomizu-dera. A ¥11,200 full-day tour covers all the above sights and includes lunch.

➤ TOUR INFORMATION: Sunrise Tours (tel. 075/341–1413).

PERSONAL GUIDES

The Japan National Tourist Organization (JNTO) sponsors a Good-Will Guide program in which local citizens volunteer to show visitors around; this is a great way to meet Japanese people. These are not professional guides; they usually volunteer both because they enjoy welcoming foreigners to their town and because they want to practice their English. The services of Good-Will Guides are free, but you should pay for their travel costs, their admission fees, and any meals you eat together. To participate in this program, make arrangements for a Good-Will Guide in advance through JNTO in the United States or through the Tourist Information Center. Within Kyōto, make arrangements one day in advance.

Contact Joe Okada at Kyōto Specialist Guide Group or consider hiring an English-speaking taxi driver to be your guide from MK Taxi.

➤ **TOUR INFORMATION: Kyōto Specialist Guide Group** (tel. 0773/64–0033). **MK Taxi** (tel. 075/721–2237).

SPECIAL-INTEREST TOURS
Kyōto Specialist Guide Group conducts special tours of Kyōto and arranges home visits for individuals and groups. Contact Joe Okada, who will tailor your tour to fit your interests and budget. Private tours are more expensive, so it's best to assemble a group if possible. The Tourist Section of the Department of Cultural Affairs and Tourism can arrange home visits.

➤ **TOUR INFORMATION: Kyōto Specialist Guide Group** (tel. 0773/64–0033). **Tourist Section, Department of Cultural Affairs and Tourism** (Kyōto City Government, Kyōto Kaikan, Okazaki, Sakyō-ku, tel. 075/752–0215).

WALKING TOURS
The Japan National Tourist Office (JNTO) publishes suggested walking routes, which offer maps and brief descriptions for five tours, ranging in length from about 40 minutes to 80 minutes. The walking-tour brochures are available from the JNTO's Tourist Information Center (☞ Visitor Information, *below*) at the Kyōto Tower Building in front of Kyōto Eki. Personable

Kyōtoite Johnnie Hajime Hirooka conducts walking tours of Kyōto, in English, that leave from Kyōto Eki at 10:15 AM Monday–Thursday, early March–late November, rain or shine. Itineraries vary—he often takes people to sights they might not otherwise see. Walks last four hours and cost ¥2,000 per person, ¥3,000 per couple.

➤ **TOUR INFORMATION: Johnnie Hajime Hirooka** (tel./fax 075/ 622–6803).

Subway Travel

Kyōto has a 26-station subway system. The Karasuma Line runs north to south from Kokusai Kaikan to Takeda. The Tōzai Line runs between Nijō in the west and Daigo in the east. Purchase tickets at the vending machines in stations before boarding. Fares increase with distance traveled and begin at ¥200. Service runs 5:30 AM–11:30 PM. Discounted passes are available for tourists (☞ Bus Travel Within Kyōto).

Taxes

HOTEL
A 5% national consumption tax is added to all hotel bills. Another 3% local tax is added to the bill if it exceeds ¥15,000. You may **save money by paying for your hotel meals separately** rather than charging them to your bill.

At first-class, full-service, and luxury hotels, a 10% service charge is added to the bill in place of individual tipping. At the more expensive ryokan, where individualized maid service is offered, the service charge is usually 15%. At business hotels, minshuku, youth hostels, and economy inns, no service charge is added to the bill.

SALES
There is an across-the-board, nonrefundable 5% consumer tax levied on all sales. Vendors either absorb the tax in their quoted

retail prices or add it on to the sale. A 5% federal consumer tax is added to all restaurant bills. Another 3% local tax is added to the bill if it exceeds ¥7,500. At the more expensive restaurants, a 10%–15% service charge is added to the bill. Tipping is not customary.

Taxis

Taxis are readily available in Kyōto. They're also expensive. Fares for smaller-size cabs start at ¥650 for the first 2 km (1 mi), with a cost of ¥90 for each additional ⅓ km (⅓ mi). Many taxi companies provide guided tours of the city, priced per hour or per route. Keihan Taxi has four-hour tours from ¥14,600 per car; MK Taxi runs similar tours for ¥16,600. There are fixed fares for some sightseeing services that start and end at Kyōto Eki. A 7½-hour tour of the city's major sights will cost ¥26,000 with any of 17 taxi companies, including Keihan Taxi and MK Taxi.

In general, it's easy to hail a cab: simply **raise your hand if you need a taxi.** Japanese taxis have automatic door-opening systems, so **do not try to open the taxi door.** Stand back when the cab comes to a stop—if you are too close, the door may slam into you. When you leave the cab, do not try to close the door; the driver will do it automatically. Only the curbside rear door opens. A red light on the dashboard indicates an available taxi, and a green light indicates an occupied taxi.

Drivers are for the most part courteous, although sometimes they balk at the idea of a foreign passenger because they do not speak English. Unless you are going to a well-known destination such as a major hotel, it is advisable to **have a Japanese person write out your destination in Japanese.** Remember, there is no need to tip.

➤ **LOCAL COMPANIES: Keihan Taxi** (tel. 0120/113–103). **MK Taxi** (tel. 075/721–2237).

Telephones

AREA & COUNTRY CODES

The country code for Japan is 81. When dialing a Japanese number from outside of Japan, drop the initial 0 from the local area code. The country code is 1 for the United States and Canada, 61 for Australia, 64 for New Zealand, and 44 for the United Kingdom.

DIRECTORY & OPERATOR ASSISTANCE

Operator assistance at 104 is in Japanese only. Weekdays 9–5 (except national holidays), English-speaking operators can help you at the toll-free NTT Information Customer Service Centre.

➤ **CONTACTS: Directory Assistance** (tel. 104). **NTT Information Customer Service Centre** (tel. 0120/364–463).

INTERNATIONAL CALLS

Many gray, multicolor, and green phones have gold plates indicating, in English, that they can be used for international calls. Three Japanese companies provide international service: KDDI (001), Japan Telecom (0041), and IDC (0061). Dial the company code + country code + city/area code and number of your party. KDD offers the clearest connection but is also the most expensive. Telephone credit cards are especially convenient for international calls. For operator assistance in English for long-distance calls, dial 0051.

LONG-DISTANCE SERVICES

AT&T, MCI, and Sprint access codes make calling long distance relatively convenient, but you may find the local access number blocked in many hotel rooms. First ask the hotel operator to connect you. If the hotel operator balks, ask for an international operator, or dial the international operator yourself. One way to improve your odds of getting connected to your long-distance carrier is to travel with more than one company's calling card (a hotel may block Sprint, for example, but not MCI). If all else fails, call from a pay phone.

➤ **ACCESS CODES:** For local access numbers abroad, contact one of the following: **AT&T Direct** (tel. 800/222–0300). **MCI WorldPhone** (tel. 800/444–4444). **Sprint International Access** (tel. 800/877–4646).

PUBLIC PHONES

Pay phones are one of the great delights of Japan. Not only are they conveniently located in hotels, restaurants, and on street corners, but at ¥10 for three minutes, they have to be one of the few remaining bargains in Japan.

Telephones come in various colors, including pink, red, and green. Most pink and red phones, for local calls, accept only ¥10 coins. Green and gray phones accept ¥10 and ¥100 coins as well as prepaid telephone cards. Domestic long-distance rates are reduced as much as 50% after 9 PM (40% after 7 PM). Green phones take coins and accept telephone cards—disposable cards of fixed value that you use up in increments of ¥10. Telephone cards, sold in vending machines, hotels, and a variety of stores, are tremendously convenient because you will not have to search for the correct change.

Time

Kyōto is 9 hours ahead of Greenwich Mean Time and 14 hours ahead of U.S. Eastern Standard Time. Daylight saving time is not observed.

Tipping

Tipping is not common in Japan. It's not necessary to tip taxi drivers, or at hair salons, barbershops, bars, or nightclubs. A chauffeur for a hired car usually receives a tip of ¥500 for a half-day excursion and ¥1,000 for a full-day trip. Porters charge fees of ¥250–¥300 per bag at railroad stations and ¥200 per piece at airports. It's not customary to tip employees of hotels, even porters, unless a special service has been rendered. In such cases, a gratuity of ¥2,000 or ¥3,000 should be placed in an envelope and handed to the staff member discreetly.

Tours & Packages

Because everything is prearranged on a prepackaged tour or independent vacation, you spend less time planning—and often get it all at a good price.

BOOKING WITH AN AGENT

Travel agents are excellent resources. But it's a good idea to collect brochures from several agencies as some agents' suggestions may be influenced by relationships with tour and package firms that reward them for volume sales. If you have a special interest, **find an agent with expertise in that area**; the American Society of Travel Agents (ASTA; ☞ Travel Agencies) has a database of specialists worldwide.

Make sure your travel agent knows the accommodations and other services of the place being recommended. Ask about the hotel's location, room size, beds, and whether it has a pool, room service, or programs for children, if you care about these. Has your agent been there in person or sent others whom you can contact?

Do some homework on your own, too: local tourism boards can provide information about lesser-known and small-niche operators, some of which may sell only direct.

BUYER BEWARE

Each year consumers are stranded or lose their money when tour operators—even large ones with excellent reputations—go out of business. So **check out the operator**. Ask several travel agents about its reputation, and try to **book with a company that has a consumer-protection program**. (Look for information in the company's brochure.) In the United States, members of the National Tour Association and the United States Tour

Operators Association are required to set aside funds to cover your payments and travel arrangements in the event that the company defaults. It's also a good idea to choose a company that participates in the American Society of Travel Agents' Tour Operator Program (TOP); ASTA will act as mediator in any disputes between you and your tour operator.

Remember that the more your package or tour includes the better you can predict the ultimate cost of your vacation. Make sure you know exactly what is covered, and **beware of hidden costs**. Are taxes, tips, and transfers included? Entertainment and excursions? These can add up.

➤ **TOUR-OPERATOR RECOMMENDATIONS: American Society of Travel Agents** (☞ Travel Agencies). **National Tour Association** (NTA; 546 E. Main St., Lexington, KY 40508, tel. 859/226–4444 or 800/682–8886, www.ntaonline.com). **United States Tour Operators Association** (USTOA; 342 Madison Ave., Suite 1522, New York, NY 10173, tel. 212/599–6599 or 800/468–7862, fax 212/599–6744, www.ustoa.com).

Train Travel

Efficient and convenient, trains run frequently and on schedule. The Shinkansen (bullet train), one of the fastest trains in the world, connects major cities north and south of Tōkyō. It is only slightly less expensive than flying but is in many ways more convenient because train stations are more centrally located than airports (and, if you have a Japan Rail Pass ☞ Cutting Costs, it's extremely affordable).

Frequent daily Shinkansen run between Tōkyō and Kyōto (2 hours, 40 minutes). The one-way fare, including charges for a reserved seat, is ¥13,220. Train service between Ōsaka and Kyōto (30 minutes) costs ¥540 one-way. From Shin-Ōsaka Eki, you can take the Shinkansen and be in Kyōto in 15 minutes;

tickets cost ¥1,380. You may use a Japan Rail Pass on the Hikari and Kodama Shinkansen.

The Keihan and the Hankyū limited express trains (40 minutes each) are less expensive than the JR, unless you have a JR Pass. The one-way Ōsaka–Kyōto fare is ¥400 or ¥460 on the Keihan Line and ¥390 on the Hankyū Line. They depart every 15 minutes from Ōsaka's Yodoyabashi and Umeda stations respectively.

In Kyōto, the Keihan Line from Ōsaka is partly underground (from Shichijō Eki to Demachi-Yanagi Eki) and extends all the way up the east bank of the Kamo-gawa to Imadegawa-dōri. At Imadegawa-dōri a passage connects the Keihan Line with the Eizan Railway's Demachi-Yanagi Eki. The Eizan has two lines, the Kurama Line, running north to Kurama, and the Eizan Line, running northeast to Yase. The Hankyū Line, which runs to the Katsura Rikyū, connects with the subway at Karasuma Eki. From Shijō-Ōmiya Eki the Keifuku Arashiyama Line runs to western Kyōto. JR also runs to western Kyōto on the San-in Main Line.

CUTTING COSTS

If you plan to travel by rail through Japan, **get a Japan Rail Pass,** which offers unlimited travel on Japan Railways (JR) trains. You can purchase one-, two-, or three-week passes. A one-week pass is less expensive than a regular round-trip ticket from Tōkyō to Kyōto on the Shinkansen. You must **obtain a rail pass voucher prior to departure for Japan** (you cannot buy them in Japan), and the pass must be used within three months of purchase. The pass is available only to people with tourist visas, as opposed to business, student, and diplomatic visas.

When you arrive in Japan, you must exchange your voucher for the Japan Rail Pass. You can do this at the Japan Railways desk in the arrivals hall at Narita Airport or at the JR stations of major cities. When you make this exchange, you determine the day that you want the rail pass to begin, and, accordingly, when it ends. You do not have to begin travel on the day you make the exchange; instead, **pick the starting date to maximize use.** The Japan Rail Pass allows you to travel on all JR-operated trains (which cover most destinations in Japan) but not lines owned by other companies.

The JR Pass is also valid on buses operated by Japan Railways. You can make seat reservations without paying a fee on all trains that have reserved-seat coaches, usually the long-distance trains. The Japan Rail Pass does not cover the cost of sleeping compartments on overnight trains (called blue trains), nor does it cover the newest and fastest of the Shinkansen trains, the Nozomi.

Japan Rail Passes are available in coach class and first class (Green Car), but most people find that coach class is more than adequate. A one-week pass costs ¥28,300 coach class, ¥37,800 first class; a two-week pass costs ¥45,100 coach class, ¥61,200 first class; and a three-week pass costs ¥57,700 coach class, ¥79,600 first class. Travelers under 18 pay lower rates. The pass pays for itself after one Tōkyō–Kyōto round-trip Shinkansen ride. Contact a travel agent or Japan Airlines to purchase the pass.

➤ **INFORMATION: Japan Railways Group** (1 Rockefeller Plaza, Suite 1622, New York, NY 10020, tel. 212/332–8686, fax 212/332–8690).

➤ **BUYING A PASS: Japan Airlines** (JAL; 655 5th Ave., New York, NY 10022 USA, tel. 212/838–4400). **Japan Travel Bureau** (JTB; 810 7th Ave., 34th floor, New York, NY 10019, tel. 212/698–4900 or 800/223–6104). **Nippon Travel Agency** (NTA; 111 Pavonia Ave., Suite 317, Jersey City, NJ 07310, tel. 201/420–6000 or 800/682–7872).

FARES & SCHEDULES
➤ **TRAIN INFORMATION: JR Hotline** English-language information service (tel. 03/3423–0111), open weekdays 10–6.

RESERVATIONS
If you're using a rail pass, there's no need to buy individual tickets, but you should **book seats ahead.** This guarantees you a

seat and is also a useful reference for the times of train departures and arrivals. You can reserve up to two weeks in advance or just minutes before the train departs. If you fail to make a train, there is no penalty, and you can reserve again.

Seat reservations for any JR route may be made at most JR stations. The reservation windows or offices, *midori-no-madoguchi*, have green signs in English and green-stripe windows. If you're traveling without a Japan Rail Pass, there's a surcharge of approximately ¥500 (depending upon distance traveled) for seat reservations, and if you miss the train, you'll have to pay for another reservation. Your reservation ticket shows the date and departure time of your train as well as your car and seat number. If you don't have a reservation, ask which cars are unreserved. Sleeping berths, even with a rail pass, are additional. Unreserved tickets can be purchased at regular ticket windows. There are no reservations made on local service trains. For traveling short distances, tickets are usually sold at vending machines.

Most clerks at train stations know a few basic words of English and can read roman script. Moreover, they are invariably helpful in plotting your route. The complete railway timetable is a mammoth book written only in Japanese; however, you can get **an English-language train schedule from the Japan National Tourist Organization** (JNTO; ☞ Visitor Information) that covers the Shinkansen and a few of the major JR Limited Express trains. JNTO's booklet *The Tourist's Handbook* provides helpful information about purchasing tickets in Japan.

Travel Agencies

A good travel agent puts your needs first. Look for an agency that has been in business at least five years, emphasizes customer service, and has someone on staff who specializes in your destination. In addition, **make sure the agency belongs to a** professional trade organization. The American Society of Travel Agents (ASTA)—the largest and most influential in the field with more than 26,000 members in some 170 countries—maintains and enforces a strict code of ethics and will step in to help mediate any agent-client disputes if necessary. ASTA (whose motto is "Without a travel agent, you're on your own") also maintains a Web site that includes a directory of agents. (If a travel agency is also acting as your tour operator, *see* Buyer Beware in Tours & Packages)

➤ **LOCAL AGENT REFERRALS: American Society of Travel Agents** (ASTA; 1101 King St., Suite 200, Alexandria, VA 22314, tel. 800/965–2782 24-hr hot line, fax 703/739–7642, www.astanet.com). **Association of British Travel Agents** (68–71 Newman St., London W1T 3AH, tel. 020/7637–2444, fax 020/7637–0713, www.abtanet. com). **Association of Canadian Travel Agents** (130 Albert St., Suite 1705, Ottawa, Ontario K1P 5G4, tel. 613/237–3657, fax 613/237–7052, www.acta.net). **Australian Federation of Travel Agents** (Level 3, 309 Pitt St., Sydney NSW 2000, tel. 02/9264–3299, fax 02/9264–1085, www.afta.com.au). **Travel Agents' Association of New Zealand** (Level 5, Paxus House, 79 Boulcott St., Box 1888, Wellington 10033, tel. 04/499–0104, fax 04/499–0827, www. taanz.org.nz).

Visitor Information

For information before you go, contact the Japan National Tourist Organization (JNTO). You may also want to check out its Web site at www.jnto.go.jp. The Japan National Tourist Organization's (JNTO) Tourist Information Center (TIC) is in the Kyōto Tower Building, in front of JR Kyōto Eki. (Take the Karasuma exit, on the side opposite the Shinkansen tracks.) Japan Travel Phone, a nationwide English-language information line for visitors, is available 9–5 daily, year-round. It's run out of the same office as the TIC.

The Japan Travel Bureau (JTB) and Keihan Travel Agency provide information on tours, such as the Sunrise Tours JTB offers; conferences and symposiums; and obtaining Japan Rail Passes. The JTB Web site lists contact numbers outside of Japan.

The Kyōto city government operates a tourist-information office in the Kyōto Eki Building; it's open daily 8:30–7.

➤ **JAPAN NATIONAL TOURIST ORGANIZATION (JNTO): Canada:** (165 University Ave., Toronto, Ontario M5H 3B8, tel. 416/366–7140). **Japan:** (2–10–1 Yūrakuchō 1-chōme, Chiyoda-ku, Tōkyō, tel. 03/3502–1461; Kyōto Tower Bldg., Higashi-Shiokoji-chō, Shimogyo-ku, Kyōto, tel. 075/371–5649). **United Kingdom:** (Heathcoat House, 20 Savile Row, London W1X 1AE, tel. 020/7734–9638). **United States:** (1 Rockefeller Plaza, Suite 1250, New York, NY 10020, tel. 212/757–5640; 401 N. Michigan Ave., Suite 770, Chicago, IL 60611, tel. 312/222–0874; 1 Daniel Burnham Court, San Francisco, CA 94109, tel. 415/292–5686; 515 S. Figueroa St., Suite 1470, Los Angeles, CA 90071, tel. 213/623–1952).

➤ **TOURIST INFORMATION IN KYŌTO: Japan Travel Bureau** (Kyōto Eki-mae, Shiokōji Karasuma Higashi-Iru, Shimogyō-ku, tel. 075/361–7241, www.jtb.co.jp/engl). **Japan Travel Phone** (tel. 075/371–5649). **Keihan Travel Agency** (12 Mori-chō, Fushimi-ku, tel. 075/602–8162). **Kyōto City Government** (Kyōto Eki Bldg., Higashi-Shiokōji-chō, Shimogyō-ku, tel. 075/343–6655). **Tourist Information Center** (Karasuma-dōri, Higashi-Shiokōji-chō, Shimogyō-ku, tel. 075/371–5649).

Web Sites

Do check out the World Wide Web when planning your trip. You'll find everything from weather forecasts to virtual tours of famous cities. Be sure to visit **Fodors.com** (www.fodors.com), a complete travel-planning site. You can research prices and book plane tickets, hotel rooms, rental cars, vacation packages, and more.

Cultural resources and travel-planning tools abound for the cybertraveler to Japan. Good first stops include the Web sites of Japan's two major English-language daily newspapers, the *Daily Yomiuri* and the *Japan Times*. For travel updates, visit the Web site of the Japan National Tourist Office (JNTO).

Visit Business Insight Japan's invaluable "Expert on Travel Planner." You enter the town from which you're departing and your destination, and the planner presents you with the travel time, fare, and distance for all possible routes. Japan Rail's sites are handy planning tools as well, and provide fare and ticket information. Both the JR East and the JR West sites will direct you to detailed information about the Japan Rail Pass (☞ Train Travel).

On the Web site of the Japan City Hotel Association, you can search member hotels by location and price and make reservations on-line. Japan Economy Hotels Reservation Service, Inc., is another on-line lodging resource.

Japanese-Online is a series of on-line language lessons. Kabuki for Everyone provides a comprehensive and accessible introduction to the dramatic form.

➤ **URLS: Business Insight Japan** (www.businessinsightjapan. com). *Daily Yomiuri* (www.yomiuri.co.jp/index-e.htm). **Japan City Hotel Association** (jcha.yadojozu.ne.jp/english/index.htm). **Japan Economy Hotels Reservation Service, Inc.** (www.inn-info. co.jp/english/home.html). **Japan National Tourist Office** (www.jnto.go.jp). **Japan Rail East** (www.jreast.co.jp/e). **Japan Rail West** (www.westjr.co.jp/kou/english/index.html). **Japan Times** (www.japantimes.co.jp). **Japanese-Online** (www.japanese-online.com). **Kabuki for Everyone** (www.fix. co.jp/kabuki/kabuki.html).

When to Go

For the most part, the climate of Japan is temperate and resembles that of the east coast of the United States. The best seasons to travel to Kyōto are spring and fall, when the weather is best. In the spring, the country is warm, with only occasional showers, and flowers grace landscapes in both rural and urban areas. The first harbingers of spring are plum blossoms in early March; *sakura* (cherry blossoms) follow some time in early April. Summer brings on the rainy season, with particularly heavy rains and humidity in July. Fall is a welcome relief, with clear blue skies and glorious foliage. Occasionally a few brief surprise typhoons occur in early fall. Winter is gray and chilly, with little snow in most areas.

To avoid crowds, **do not plan a trip for times when most Japanese are vacationing.** For the most part, Japanese cannot select when they want to take their vacations; they tend to do so on the same holiday dates. As a result, airports, planes, trains, and hotels are booked far in advance. Many businesses, shops, and restaurants are closed during these holidays. Holiday periods include the few days before and after New Year's; Golden Week, which follows Greenery Day (April 29); and mid-August at the time of the Obon festivals, when many Japanese return to their hometowns.

CLIMATE

The following is a list of average daily maximum and minimum temperatures for Kyōto.

KYŌTO

Jan.	48F	9C	May	75F	24C	Sept.	82F	28C
	35	2		56	13		68	20
Feb.	53F	12C	June	82F	28C	Oct.	74F	23C
	32	0		66	19		53	12
Mar.	59F	15C	July	93F	34C	Nov.	62F	17C
	40	4		72	22		46	8
Apr.	65F	18C	Aug.	89F	32C	Dec.	53F	12C
	44	7		74	23		33	1

AN ENGLISH-JAPANESE TRAVELER'S VOCABULARY

Japanese sounds and spellings differ in principle from those of the West. We build words letter by letter, and one letter can sound different depending where it appears in a word. For example, we see *ta* as two letters, and *ta* could be pronounced three ways, as in *tat*, *tall*, and *tale*. For the Japanese, *ta* is one character, and it is pronounced one way: *tah*.

The *hiragana* and *katakana* (tables of sounds) are the rough equivalents of our alphabet. There are four types of syllables within these tables: the single vowels *a*, *i*, *u*, *e*, and *o*, in that order; vowel-consonant pairs like *ka*, *ni*, *hu*, or *ro*; the single consonant *n*, which punctuates the upbeats of the word for bullet train, *Shinkansen* (*shee-n-ka-n-se-n*); and compounds like *kya*, *chu*, and *ryo*. Remember that these compounds are one syllable. Thus Tōkyō, the capital city has only two syllables—*tō* and *kyō*—not three. Likewise pronounce Kyōtō *kyō-tō*, not *kee-oh-to*.

Japanese vowels are pronounced as follows: *a–ah*, *i–ee*, *u–oo*, *e–eh*, *o–oh*. The Japanese *r* is rolled so that it sounds like a bounced *d*.

No diphthongs. Paired vowels in Japanese words are not slurred together, as in our words *coin*, *brain*, or *stein*. The Japanese separate them, as in *mae* (*ma-eh*), which means in front of; *kōen* (*ko-en*), which means park; *byoin* (*byo-een*), which means hospital; and *tokei* (*to-keh-ee*), which means clock or watch.

Macrons. Many Japanese words, when rendered in *romaji* (roman letters), require macrons over vowels to indicate correct pronunciation, as in Tōkyō. When you see these macrons, double the length of the vowel, as if you're saying it twice: *to-o-kyo-o*. Likewise, when you see double consonants, as in the city name Nikkō, linger on the Ks—as in "bookkeeper"—and on the O.

Emphasis. Some books state that the Japanese emphasize all syllables in their words equally. This is not true. Take the words *sayōnara* and *Hiroshima*. Americans are likely to stress the downbeats: sa-yo-na-ra and hi-ro-shi-ma. The Japanese actually emphasize the second beat in each case: sa-yō-na-ra (note the macron) and hi-ro-shi-ma. Metaphorically speaking, the Japanese don't so much stress syllables as pause over them or race past them: Emphasis is more a question of speed than weight. In the vocabulary below, we indicate emphasis by italicizing the syllable that you should stress.

Three interesting pronunciations are in the vocabulary below. The word *desu* roughly means "is." It looks like it has two syllables, but the Japanese race past the final u and just say "dess." Likewise, some verbs end in -*masu*, which is pronounced "mahss." Similarly, the character *shi* is often quickly pronounced "sh," as in the phrase meaning "pleased to meet you:" ha-ji-me-mash(i)-te. Just like *desu* and -*masu*, what look like two syllables, in this case, *ma* and *shi*, are pronounced *mahsh*.

Hyphens. We have hyphenated certain words to help you recognize meaningful patterns. This isn't conventional; it is practical. For example, *Eki-mae-dōri*, which literally means "Station Front Avenue," turns into a blur when rendered Ekimaedōri. And in the Kyōto chapter, where you'll run across a number of sight names that end in -*jingū* or -*jinja* or -*taisha*, you'll soon catch on to their meaning: Shintō shrine.

Glossary. In the same spirit, we have added a glossary to the Introducing Kyōto chapter to signal important words. Knowing these few words and suffixes adds meaning to reading about Japan and makes asking directions from Japanese people a whole lot more productive.

Basics　基本的表現

Yes/No	*ha-i*/*ii-e*	はい／いいえ
Please	o-ne-*gai* shi-masu	お願いします
Thank you (very much)	(*dō*-mo) a-*ri*-ga-to go-*zai*-ma su	(どうも)ありがとう ございます
You're welcome	*dō* i-ta-shi-ma-shi-te	どういたしまして
Excuse me	su-mi-ma-*sen*	すみません
Sorry	go-men na-*sai*	ごめんなさい
Good morning	o-*ha*-yō go-zai-ma-su	お早うございます
Good day/afternoon	kon-*ni*-chi-wa	こんにちは
Good evening	kom-*ban*-wa	こんばんは
Good night	o-*ya*-su-mi na-*sai*	おやすみなさい
Goodbye	sa-*yō*-na-ra	さようなら
Mr./Mrs./Miss	-san	―さん
Pleased to meet you	*ha*-ji-me-*mashi*-te	はじめまして
How do you do?	*dō*-zo yo-*ro*-shi-ku	どうぞよろしく

Numbers　数

The first reading is used for reading numbers, as in telephone numbers, and the second is often used for counting things.

1	*i*-chi / hi-*to*-tsu	一／一つ	17	*jū*-shi-chi	十七
2	ni / fu-*ta*-tsu	二／二つ	18	*jū*-ha-chi	十八
3	san / *mit*-tsu	三／三つ	19	*jū*-kyū	十九
4	shi / *yot*-tsu	四／四つ	20	*ni*-jū	二十
5	go / i-*tsu*-tsu	五／五つ	21	*ni*-jū-i-chi	二十一
6	*ro*-ku / *mut*-tsu	六／六つ	30	*san*-jū	三十
7	*na*-na / *na*-na-tsu	七／七つ	40	*yon*-jū	四十
8	*ha*-chi / *yat*-tsu	八／八つ	50	*go*-jū	五十
9	kyū / *ko*-ko-no-*tsu*	九／九つ	60	*ro*-ku-jū	六十
10	jū / tō	十／十	70	na-na-jū	七十
11	*jū*-i-chi	十一	80	*ha*-chi-jū	八十
12	*jū*-ni	十二	90	kyū-jū	九十
13	*jū*-san	十三	100	*hya*-ku	百
14	*jū*-yon	十四	1000	sen	千
15	*jū*-go	十五	10,000	*i*-chi-man	一万
16	*jū*-ro-ku	十六	100,000	*jū*-man	十万

Days of the Week 曜日

Sunday	*ni*-chi yō-bi	日曜日
Monday	*ge*-tsu yō-bi	月曜日
Tuesday	*ka* yō-bi	火曜日
Wednesday	*su*-i yō-bi	水曜日
Thursday	*mo*-ku yō-bi	木曜日
Friday	*kin* yō-bi	金曜日
Saturday	*dō* yō-bi	土曜日
Weekday	hei-ji-tsu	平日
Weekend	Shū-ma-tsu	週末

Months 月

January	*i*-chi *ga*-tsu	一月
February	*ni* ga-tsu	二月
March	*san* ga-tsu	三月
April	*shi* ga-tsu	四月
May	go ga-tsu	五月
June	*ro*-ku *ga*-tsu	六月
July	*shi*-chi *ga*-tsu	七月
August	*ha*-chi *ga*-tsu	八月
September	*ku* ga-tsu	九月
October	*jū* ga-tsu	十月
November	*jū*-i-chi *ga*-tsu	十一月
December	*jū*-ni *ga*-tsu	十二月

Useful Expressions, Questions, and Answers よく使われる表現

Do you speak English?	*ei*-go ga wa-*ka*-ri-ma-su *ka*	英語が。わかりますか
I don't speak Japanese.	*ni*-hon-go ga wa-*ka*-ri-ma-*sen*	日本語がわかりません。
I don't understand.	wa-*ka*-ri-ma-*sen*	わかりません。
I understand.	wa-*ka*-ri-ma-shi-*ta*	わかりました。
I don't know.	*shi*-ri-ma-*sen*	知りません。
I'm American (British)	wa-*ta*-shi wa a-*me*-ri-ka (i-*gi*-ri-su) jin *desu*	私はアメリカ（イギリス）人です。
What's your name?	o-*na*-ma-e wa *nan* desu *ka*	お名前は何ですか。
My name is . . .	. . . to *mo*-shi-*ma*-su	……と申します。
What time is it?	*i*-ma *nan*-ji desu *ka*	今何時ですか。

How?	*dō* yat-te	どうやって。
When?	*i*-tsu	いつ。
Yesterday/today/tomorrow	ki-*nō*/kyō/*ashi*-ta	きのう／きょう／あした
This morning	*ke*-sa	けさ
This afternoon	*kyō* no *go*-go	きょうの午後
Tonight	*kom*-ban	こんばん
Excuse me, what?	su-*mi*-ma-*sen, nan* desu *ka*	すみません、何ですか。
What is this/that?	*ko*-re/*so*-re wa *nan* desu *ka*	これ／それは何ですか。
Why?	*na*-ze desu *ka*	なぜですか。
Who?	*da*-re desu *ka*	だれですか。
I am lost.	*mi*-chi ni ma-yo-i-*mash*-ta	道に迷いました。
Where is [place]	[place] wa *do*-ko desu *ka*	.....はどこですか。
Train station?	e-ki	駅
Subway station?	chi-*ka*-te-tsu-no eki	地下鉄の駅
Bus stop?	*ba*-su *no*-ri-*ba*	バス乗り場
Taxi stand?	*ta*-ku-shi-i *no*-ri-*ba*	タクシー乗り場
Airport?	kū-kō	空港
Post office?	*yū*-bin-*kyo*-ku	郵便局
Bank?	*gin*-kō	銀行
the [name] hotel?	[name] ho-*te*-ru	ホテル
Elevator?	e-re-bē-tā	エレベーター
Where are the restrooms?	*to*-i-re wa *do*-ko desu *ka*	トイレはどこですか。
Here/there/over there	*ko*-ko/*so*-ko/*a*-so-ko	ここ／そこ／あそこ
Left/right	hi-*da*-ri/*mi*-gi	左／右
Straight ahead	mas-*su*-gu	まっすぐ
Is it near (far)?	chi-*ka*-i (*to*-i) desu *ka*	近い（遠い）ですか。
Are there any rooms?	*he*-ya *ga* a-ri-masu *ka*	部屋がありますか。
I'd like [item]	[item] ga ho-*shi*-i no desu *ga*	.....がほしいのですが。
Newspaper	*shim*-bun	新聞
Stamp	*kit*-te	切手

Key	*ka*-gi	鍵
I'd like to buy [item]	[item] o kai-*ta*-i no desu ke do	.....を買いたいのですけど。
a ticket to [event]	[event] *ma*-de no *kip*-pu	.....までの切符
Map	*chi*-zu	地図
How much is it?	i-*ku*-ra desu *ka*	いくらですか。
It's expensive (cheap).	ta-*ka*-i (ya-*su*-i) de su *ne*	高い (安い) ですね。
A little (a lot)	su-*ko*-shi (*ta*-ku-san)	少し (たくさん)
More/less	*mot*-to o-ku/ su-ku-*na*-ku	もっと多く／少なく
Enough/too much	*jū*-bun/o-su-*gi*-ru	十分／多すぎる
I'd like to exchange . . .	. . . *ryō*-ga e shi-*te* i-*ta*-da-ke-masu *ka*	.....両替して頂けますか。
dollars to yen	*do*-ru o *en* ni	ドルを円に
pounds to yen	*pon*-do o *en* ni	ポンドを円に
How do you say . . . in Japanese?	ni-*hon*-go de . . . wa *dō* i-i-masu *ka*	日本語で....はどう言いますか。
I am ill/sick.	wa-*ta*-shi wa *byō*-ki desu	私は病気です。
Please call a doctor.	*i*-sha o *yon*-de ku-da-*sa*-i	医者を呼んで下さい。
Please call the police.	*ke*-i-sa-tsu o *yon*-de ku-da-*sa*-i	警察を呼んで下さい。
Help!	*ta*-su-*ke*-te	助けて！

Restaurants　レストラン
Basics and Useful Expressions　よく使われる表現

A bottle of . . .	. . . *ip*-pon	.....一本
A glass/cup of . . .	. . . *ip*-pai	.....一杯
Ashtray	*ha*-i-*za*-ra	灰皿
Plate	*sa*-ra	皿
Bill/check	kan-*jō*	かんじょう
Bread	pan	パン
Breakfast	*chō*-sho-ku	朝食
Butter	ba-*tā*	バター
Cheers!	kam-*pai*	乾杯！

Chopsticks	*ha*-shi	箸
Cocktail	*ka*-ku-*te*-ru	カクテル
Dinner Does that include...	*yū*-sho-ku *ga tsu-ki-ma-su-ka*	夕食が付きますか。
Excuse me!	su-mi-ma-*sen*	すみません
Fork	*fō*-ku	フォーク
I am diabetic.	wa-*ta*-shi wa tō-*nyō*-byō de su	私は糖尿病です。
I am dieting.	*da*-i-et-to *chū* desu	ダイエット中です。
I am a vegetarian.	sa-i-*sho*-ku *shū*-gi-sha de-su	菜食主義者です。
I cannot eat [item]	[item] wa *ta*-be-ra-re-ma-*sen*	.....は食べられません。
I'd like to order.	*chū*-mon o shi-*tai* desu	注文をしたいです。
I'd like [item]	[item] o o-ne-*gai*-shi-ma su	.....をお願いします。
I'm hungry.	o-na-ka ga *su*-i-te i-*ma* su	お腹が空いています。
I'm thirsty.	*no*-do ga ka-*wa*-i-te i-*ma* su	喉が渇いています。
It's tasty (not good)	*o*-i-shi-i (ma-*zu*-i) desu	おいしい（まずい）です。
Knife	*na*-i-fu	ナイフ
Lunch	*chū*-sho-ku	昼食
Menu	me-nyū	メニュー
Napkin	*na*-pu-*kin*	ナプキン
Pepper	ko-*shō*	こしょう
Please give me [item]	[item] o ku-da-*sa*-i	.....を下さい。
Salt	*shi*-o	塩
Set menu	*te*-i-sho-ku	定食
Spoon	su-*pūn*	スプーン
Sugar	sa-to	砂糖
Wine list	*wa*-i-n *ri*-su-*to*	ワインリスト
What do you recommend?	o-su-su-me *ryō*-ri wa *nan* desu ka	お勧め料理は何ですか。

Meat Dishes 肉料理

焼き肉	yaki-niku	Thinly sliced meat is marinated then barbecued over an open fire at the table.
すき焼き	suki-yaki	Thinly sliced beef, green onions, mushrooms, thin noodles, and cubes of tōfu are simmered in a large iron pan in front of you. These ingredients are cooked in a mixture of soy sauce, mirin (cooking wine), and a little sugar. You are given a saucer of raw egg to cool the suki-yaki morsels before eating. Using chopsticks, you help yourself to anything on your side of the pan and dip it into the egg and then eat. Best enjoyed in a group.
しゃぶしゃぶ	shabu-shabu	Extremely thin slices of beef are plunged for an instant into boiling water flavored with soup stock and then dipped into a thin sauce and eaten.
肉じゃが	niku-jaga	Beef and potatoes stewed together with soy sauce.
ステーキ	sutēki	steak
ハンバーグ	hambāgu	Hamburger pattie served with sauce.
トンカツ	tonkatsu	Breaded deep-fried pork cutlets.
しょうが焼	shōga-yaki	Pork cooked with ginger.
酢豚	subuta	Sweet and sour pork, originally a Chinese dish.
からあげ	kara-age	deep-fried without batter
焼き鳥	yaki-tori	Pieces of chicken, white meat, liver, skin, etc., threaded on skewers with green onions and marinated in sweet soy sauce and grilled.
親子どんぶり	oyako-domburi	Literally, "mother and child bowl"—chicken and egg in broth over rice.
他人どんぶり	tanin-domburi	Literally, "strangers in a bowl"—similar to oyako domburi, but with beef instead of chicken.

ロール・キャベツ	rōru kyabetsu	Rolled cabbage; beef or pork rolled in cabbage and cooked.
はやしライス	hayashi raisu	Beef flavored with tomato and soy sauce with onions and peas over rice.
カレーライス	karē-raisu	Curried rice. A thick curry gravy typically containing beef is poured over white rice.
カツカレー	katsu-karē	Curried rice with tonkatsu.
お好み焼き	okonomi-yaki	Sometimes called a Japanese pancake, this is made from a batter of flour, egg, cabbage, and meat or seafood, griddle-cooked then covered with green onions and a special sauce.
シュウマイ	shūmai	Shrimp or pork wrapped in a light dough and steamed.
ギョウザ	gyōza	Pork spiced with ginger and garlic in a Chinese wrapper and fried or steamed.

Seafood Dishes　魚貝類料理

焼き魚	yaki-zakana	broiled fish
塩焼	shio-yaki	Fish sprinkled with salt and broiled until crisp.
さんま	samma	saury pike
いわし	iwashi	sardines
しゃけ	shake	salmon
照り焼き	teri-yaki	Fish basted in soy sauce and broiled.
ぶり	buri	yellowtail
煮魚	nizakana	soy-simmered fish
さばのみそ煮	saba no miso ni	Mackerel stewed with soy-bean paste.
揚げ魚	age-zakana	deep-fried fish
かれいフライ	karei furai	deep-fried breaded flounder
刺身	sashimi	Very fresh raw fish. Served sliced thin on a bed of white radish with a saucer of soy sauce and horseradish. Eaten by dipping fish into soy sauce mixed with horseradish.

まぐろ	maguro	tuna
あまえび	ama-ebi	sweet shrimp
いか	ika	squid
たこ	tako	octopus
あじ	aji	horse mackerel
さわら	sawara	Spanish mackerel
しめさば	shimesaba	Mackerel marinated in vinegar.
かつおのたたき	katsuo no tataki	Bonito cooked just slightly on the surface. Eaten with cut green onions and thin soy sauce.
どじょうの柳川なべ	dojo no yanagawa nabe	Loach cooked with burdock root and egg in an earthen dish. Considered a delicacy.
うな重	una-jū	Eel marinated in a slightly sweet soy sauce is charcoal-broiled and served over rice. Considered a delicacy.
天重	ten-ju	Deep-fried prawns served over rice with sauce.
海老フライ	ebi furai	Deep-fried breaded prawns.
あさりの酒蒸し	asari no sakamushi	Clams steamed with rice wine.

Sushi 寿司

寿司	sushi	Basically, sushi is rice, fish, and vegetables. The rice is delicately seasoned with vinegar, salt, and sugar. There are basically three types of sushi: nigiri, chirashi, and maki.
にぎり寿司	nigiri zushi	The rice is formed into a bite-sized cake and topped with various raw or cooked fish. The various types are usually named after the fish, but not all are fish. Nigiri zushi is eaten by picking up the cakes with chopsticks or the fingers, dipping the fish side in soy sauce, and eating.

ちらし寿司	chirashi zushi	In chirashi zushi, a variety of seafood is arranged on the top of the rice and served in a bowl.
巻き寿司	maki zushi	Raw fish and vegetables or other morsels are rolled in sushi rice and wrapped in dried seaweed. Some popular varieties are listed here.
まぐろ	maguro	tuna
とろ	toro	fatty tuna
たい	tai	red snapper
さば	saba	mackerel
こはだ	kohada	gizzard shad
しゃけ	shake	salmon
はまち	hamachi	yellowtail
ひらめ	hirame	flounder
あじ	aji	horse mackerel
たこ	tako	octopus
あなご	anago	conger eel
えび	ebi	shrimp
甘えび	ama-ebi	sweet shrimp
いか	ika	squid
みる貝	miru-gai	giant clam
あおやぎ	aoyagi	round clam
卵	tamago	egg
かずのこ	kazunoko	herring roe
かに	kani	crab
ほたて貝	hotate-gai	scallop
うに	uni	sea urchin
いくら	ikura	salmon roe
鉄火巻	tekka-maki	tuna roll
かっぱ巻	kappa-maki	cucumber roll
新香巻	shinko-maki	shinko roll (shinko is a type of pickle)
カリフォルニア巻	kariforunia-maki	California roll, containing crab-meat and avocado. This was in-

		vented in the U.S. but was re-exported to Japan and is gaining popularity there.
うに	uni	Sea urchin on rice wrapped with seaweed.
いくら	ikura	Salmon roe on rice wrapped with seaweed.
太巻	futo-maki	Big roll with egg and pickled vegetables.

Vegetable Dishes　野菜料理

おでん	oden	Often sold by street vendors at festivals and in parks, etc., this is vegetables, octopus, or egg simmered in a soy fish stock.
天ぷら	tempura	Vegetables, shrimp, or fish deep-fried in a light batter. Eaten by dipping into a thin sauce containing grated white radish.
野菜サラダ	yasai sarada	vegetable salad
大学いも	daigaku imo	fried yams in a sweet syrup
野菜いため	yasai itame	stir-fried vegetables
きんぴらごぼう	kimpira gobō	Carrots and burdock root, fried with soy sauce.
煮もの	nimono	vegetables simmered in a soy- and sake-based sauce
かぼちゃ	kabocha	pumpkin
さといも	satoimo	taro root
たけのこ	takenoko	bamboo shoots
ごぼう	gobō	burdock root
れんこん	renkon	lotus root
酢のもの	sumono	Vegetables seasoned with ginger.
きゅうり	kyūri	cucumber
和えもの	aemono	Vegetables dressed with sauces.
ねぎ	tamanegi	onions
おひたし	o-hitashi	Boiled vegetables with soy sauce and dried shaved bonito or sesame seeds.

| ほうれん草 | hōrenso | spinach |
| 漬物 | tsukemono | Japanese pickles. Made from white radish, eggplant or other vegetables. Considered essential to the Japanese meal. |

Egg Dishes　卵料理

ベーコン・エッグ	bēkon-eggu	bacon and eggs
ハム・エッグ	hamu-eggu	ham and eggs
スクランブル・エッグ	sukuramburu eggu	scrambled eggs
ゆで卵	yude tamago	boiled eggs
目玉焼	medama-yaki	fried eggs, sunny-side up
オムレツ	omuretsu	omelet
オムライス	omuraisu	Omelet with rice inside, often eaten with ketchup.
茶わんむし	chawan mushi	Vegetables, shrimp, etc., steamed in egg custard.

Tōfu Dishes　豆腐料理

Tōfu, also called bean curd, is a white, high-protein food with the consistency of soft gelatin.

冷やっこ	hiya-yakko	Cold tōfu with soy sauce and grated ginger.
湯どうふ	yu-dōfu	boiled tōfu
あげだしどうふ	agedashi dōfu	Lightly fried plain tōfu dipped in soy sauce and grated ginger.
マーボーどうふ	mābō dōfu	Tōfu and ground pork in a spicy red sauce. Originally a Chinese dish.
とうふの田楽	tōfu no dengaku	Tōfu broiled on skewers and flavored with miso.

Rice Dishes　ごはん料理

| ごはん | gohan | steamed white rice |
| おにぎり | onigiri | Triangular balls of rice with fish or vegetables inside and wrapped in a type of seaweed. |

おかゆ	okayu	rice porridge
チャーハン	chāhan	Fried rice; includes vegetables and pork.
ちまき	chimaki	A type of onigiri made with sweet rice.
パン	pan	Bread, but usually rolls with a meal.

Soups 汁もの

みそ汁	miso shiru	Miso soup. A thin broth containing tōfu, mushrooms, or other morsels in a soup flavored with miso or soy-bean paste. The morsels are taken out of the bowl and the soup is drunk straight from the bowl without a spoon.
すいもの	suimono	Soy sauce flavored soup, often including fish and tofu.
とん汁	tonjiru	Pork soup with vegetables.

Noodles 麺類

うどん	udon	Wide flour noodles in broth. Can be lunch in a light broth or a full dinner called *nabe-yaki udon* when meat, chicken, egg, and vegetables are added.
そば	soba	Buckwheat noodles. Served in a broth like udon or, during the summer, cold on a bamboo mesh and called *zaru soba*.
ラーメン	rāmen	Chinese noodles in broth, often with *chashu* or roast pork. Broth is soy sauce, miso or salt flavored.
そう麺	sōmen	Very thin wheat noodles, usually served cold with a tsuyu or thin sauce. Eaten in summer.

index

176

FODOR'S POCKET KYŌTO

EDITOR: Deborah Kaufman

Editorial Contributors: Lauren Sheridan

Editorial Production: Stacey Kulig

Maps: David Lindroth, *cartographer;* Bob Blake and Rebecca Baer, *map editors*

Design: Fabrizio La Rocca, *creative director;* Tigist Getachew, *art director;* Melanie Marin, *photo editor*

Production/Manufacturing: Robert B. Shields

Cover Photograph: Siegfried Tauqueur/eStock Photography/PictureQuest

IMPORTANT TIP

Although all prices, opening times, and other details in this book are based on information supplied to us at press time, changes occur all the time in the travel world, and Fodor's cannot accept responsibility for facts that become outdated or for inadvertent errors or omissions. So always confirm information when it matters, especially if you're making a detour to visit a specific place.

SPECIAL SALES

Fodor's Travel Publications are available at special discounts for bulk purchases for sales promotions or premiums. Special editions, including personalized covers, excerpts of existing guides, and corporate imprints, can be created in large quantities for special needs. For more information, contact your local bookseller or write to Special Markets, Fodor's Travel Publications, 280 Park Avenue, New York, NY 10017. Inquiries from Canada should be directed to your local Canadian bookseller or sent to Random House of Canada, Ltd., Marketing Department, 2775 Matheson Boulevard East, Mississauga, Ontario L4W 4P7. Inquiries from the United Kingdom should be sent to Fodor's Travel Publications, 20 Vauxhall Bridge Road, London SW1V 2SA, England.

PRINTED IN THE UNITED STATES OF AMERICA

10 9 8 7 6 5 4 3 2 1